MELANIE HERZ PROMECENE

ISBN: 978-1-64184-282-2 (Paperback)
ISBN: 978-1-64184-281-5 (Hardcover)
ISBN: 978-1-64184-283-9 (Ebook)

Cover Design and Illustrations by Chris Promecene

This is Non-Fiction based on real-life events. Where appropriate, names have been changed out of respect for privacy.

Visit my website at www.melanieherzpromecene.com

Printed in the United States of America

Open Doors Publishing House, LLC

First Printing: 2020

For Noah, my beloved rainbow

CONTENTS

Introduction

HOW THIS BOOK CAME TO BE

When I was 8 years old, I had a secret. Sure, I had lots of secrets—pretty typical for an eight-year-old. But what I kept to myself was that I felt an overwhelming urge deep in my soul to do something big. To share an incredible adventure. Maybe even write a book one day. I remember this because of the stir I felt in my belly—like butterflies.

It's been there ever since. It was there in September 2017, when Hurricane Harvey hit Houston. During that storm, relentless rain poured from the heavens and forced its way into the house I share with my husband and our then 2 ½-year-old son.

At first, we weren't all that concerned. Our beloved mid-century modern home, built in 1963, had never flooded. We felt confident that we had food and water and wine and chocolates to last two weeks. But as the hours passed and the rain continued to pour our plans of hunkering down in place quickly subsided. In the pre-dawn hours, water began seeping into our home. By sunrise we had a foot of water.

My little family fled our home, and a great adventure began. In our terrified scramble for higher ground, we broke into our neighbor's abandoned two-story house. From the safety of the second floor, we watched boats drift down the street.

As rescue workers dropped ropes from helicopters and pulled our neighbors to safety, I wondered what would happen. *How long will we be hijacked by water? Did we stuff enough Cheese Whiz and crackers in the backpack we hastily crammed full of food and supplies as we rushed out to last a few days? Do we have enough water to stay hydrated? How much charge do we have on our phones before we disconnect from the world entirely? What will we do next?*

If it had been only me and my husband, I would have been focusing on this event as a major annoyance—a great inconvenience in a life chugging along. But our son was there, too. We were responsible for our toddler's safety, and what otherwise might have felt like an adventure became terrifying.

I also thought to myself, "We'll get through this. We're together. We're a *family*." Getting to this point had been filled with challenges and hurdles, as well as aches and pains. There was no way I was going to let something like a hurricane destroy what we had worked so long and hard to build.

After we were rescued and living life elsewhere, I found myself up every night at 3 a.m.– on the dot—reflecting. I decided to take pen to paper and jot down the thoughts circling my head. And then something miraculous happened. Words began to flow like rain. They flowed and flowed and flowed.

It started with me wanting to share the story of how my son revealed himself to us through adoption.

Actually, his spirit entered way before he did, on what I thought was the worst day of my life. It was nearly a year before Noah's birth, and I was grieving because my husband and I had decided to pass on a newborn our adoption agency presented to us. Suddenly, through my despair, a bit of hope sprang through. The butterflies in my stomach—the ones that had always told me to do something big—were telling me that my baby was on his way. Those butterflies were right: Exactly 10 months later, my son was born. The butterflies fluttered just after he was conceived. Call it a sign, call it intuition, call it a coincidence, call it a wink from God—a "Godwink"—but it was real, and it was one of many that appeared throughout the years my husband and I were trying to adopt a child.

I saw magic unfold through the exhausting adoption process. When you look at the individual events, they may seem trivial. However, as time passed, I began to see these seemingly innocent moments as the miracles they were. They gave me inspiration and propelled me forward. Some may take these experiences as faith. For me, they became confirmation that I was being guided by a Higher Power. Chris and I were not alone on our uphill journey.

When Noah was born, I promised myself that I would write this story (his story, my story, our story). I wanted him to understand where he came from and the path that brought him to us. Our adoption journey started out daunting. It became emotionally devastating and then anxiety-provoking, and finally joyous and miraculous. Getting him into our life was the most challenging and most rewarding thing his father and I have done.

My first draft of this book was entitled *Godwinks for Noah—A Mother's Journey through the Adoption Process.* What evolved was my plight with my husband, Chris, through the forest and weeds to get to Noah, our baby.

Considering the challenges I have experienced in my life to this point—from overriding my family's vision of the life I was born to lead, to overcoming innate control issues and emotional setbacks, to career path upheavals—I thought adoption would be the least of my challenges.

In the following chapters, I will tell you about the decisions, stumbling blocks and unexpected magic I discovered on my way to finding my baby. The events and experiences presented are real, but I changed many names. My story is unique but relatable. In some respects, we are all looking for meaning in a world full of chance rendezvous. By nature, we also look for ways to forge strength in times of despair. We overcome roadblocks by sheer grit and determination.

We're all on a personal quest to find that special magic that lives over the rainbow. This is my story of how I found my way to the other side of the colorful arc. Welcome.

01

Following Butterflies

Watch any teen comedy from the 1980s and you'll get a sense of what Galveston was like when I was growing up. The town was like a big high school, with every type of character you could imagine. There was the jock, the cheerleader, the class clown, the nerd, the cowboy, the stoner, the rebel.

And there was me.

I was the girl who could float from group to group. You know, that "friend" without the distinguishing *girl* beforehand. Even if everyone didn't know everyone else by name, we knew one another by sight. We knew who we were and where we fit in.

To this day, when people ask where I'm from, I smile when I say "Galveston," as we Galvestonians are quirky and colorful—by design. My roots runneth deep. I have the add-on factor of being a 5th generation Galvestonian, a true BOI (Born on the Island). This small barrier island city off the Gulf Coast of Texas is, literally, the last stop by bus or rail before the Gulf of Mexico. In the mid-19th century, its thriving port made it the Ellis Island of the South, and after landing there in the 1860s, my German *mishpocha* decided to hunker down in the cosmopolitan town of that bygone era.

Nowadays, my hometown is legendary for Glen Campbell's 1969 hit album *Galveston,* and for the notorious Robert Durst, the real estate heir and murder suspect who was the subject of a multi-state manhunt and, in the early 2000s, disguised himself as a mute woman and went into hiding on the island.

When I was a kid, before a murder suspect who pretended he couldn't talk showed up, we all thought we knew everything about everyone. Gossip and wives' tales presented themselves often, but my life was not overly dramatic. I was born in the 1970s into a very loving, tight-knit, Southern Jewish family. My father was a high-profile lawyer and my mother was a well-known fundraiser for philanthropic causes within the community. They still are. I have one slightly older brother, and we grew up learning all the proper etiquette and social protocol.

There were some bumps during my early years, but whose life doesn't have a few bruises? School was pretty easy for me until my sophomore year of high school, when geometry entered my life. I received my first C and was devastated. I pushed myself to be at the top of my class, and grades offered me a chance to feel a sense of control. Eating did, too. I soon realized that being the valedictorian, student body president, and homecoming queen were not in my cards (though I did make homecoming court all four years). I fell to number 7 in a class of 429 by my senior year, and by age 18, I struggled with what came to be the first of many major depressions.

For those not in my shoes, my life probably appeared on the more idyllic side—loving, financially stable family, great network of friends, class leader—pretty steady stuff, right? In reality, my senior year of high school was a mess. I recall visiting Gerlands grocery store with my mom and, while waiting for her to check out, I casually glanced through the magazine racks. My eyes stopped on an article geared toward teens and those struggling with eating disorders and depression. This article was my wake-up call to the disaster I was experiencing inside.

I closed the magazine, threw it into the shopping cart before check-out, and read it a dozen times before calling my mom into my room that evening. I knew I needed help but didn't know how to address it with my family. This magazine was my way out—the pages would talk for me. I left the article open to the list of symptoms and checked all that applied to me, which ended up being the full 8 ½-by-11 2-page spread, minus one or two things.

That's the moment I finally surrendered to myself, my family and a plethora of psychologists and psychiatrists. It was fall 1991 and college was around the corner. I could barely focus from week to week, much less prepare for the SAT required for college. Fortunately, my class ranking was high enough that I could just grab a No. 2 pencil and fill in the bubbles on the in-state college applications. And that's just what I did. I kept moving forward, one bubble at a time.

College expectations were programmed from birth. Like my mother and her mother, I would attend the University of Texas at Austin and rush their same sorority. I expected that, like my mother and grandmother, I'd meet my husband in college, settle down, and start a family. This vision was instilled in me at a very young age. My story, however, is different.

I struggled through my first couple years of college. Aside from the weekly therapy sessions, which actually helped stabilize me, fitting into a new world of college life and social networks was stressful. In hindsight, I wish I had been a little more carefree those first years. Eventually I hit my stride and had fun, making friendships that are as strong today as they were when we graduated over 20 years ago.

By my junior year, I found my rhythm and focus as a double major in psychology and social work. I would become a family therapist. In 1997 I graduated with a bachelor's in psychology.

Social Work was a 5-year program, so the summer between my fourth and fifth years, I journeyed to England, where I interned in a leading private psychiatric hospital. It was here, in this psychologically turbulent, unsupervised Freudian-based program that

I determined family therapy was not my path. I was too much of an empath to continue in the profession. I had a tendency to put myself in a patient's position and feel their aching energy. It was emotionally draining. My breaking point came when I saw a patient writing with feces on a wall. I knew I had to switch careers.

Until that point, my life had been carefully planned. Now that I didn't know what I was going to do next, I recoiled. Another depression set in and I was paralyzed. Getting through that final year was a struggle. Most of my friends in the 4-year program had graduated, and I was left with little support and less purpose. I persevered because I didn't know what else to do. One evening during this period, my roommate asked me to join her at a movie and I went along for the ride. It was now April 1998. I was living in Houston interning at a local elementary school. In one month, I would complete my second college degree, and I was as unsure and stressed about my next steps in life as ever.

I remember sitting in the dark movie theater and getting lost in my own thoughts. To this day I have no idea what I sat through for 2.5 hours. What I came to realize in that dim theater was that I was going to live by the seat of my pants, my head shouted, "Let's move to New York City!"

After the movie ended, I blurted to myself, "New York City? Really?" My roommate thought I was crazy. But the butterflies in my stomach were stirring and I was excited about the adventure and possibilities that awaited. "Why not?" I thought.

A month later, I was off to Manhattan. I had no place to live, no job, and no idea what would come next. For the first time ever, I was exuberant about the unexpected. It was a good thing my college friends Dorey, Laura, and Anne were living in the City. I had sofas to sleep on until I could land on my feet.

New York City awakened my soul and I felt completely uninhibited for the first time in my life. I was in my 20s and having a blast. This magical city is where I grew up and metamorphized into the person I am today. I found my calling in the arts and enrolled at Parsons School of Design. I finally had a path forward: interior design.

I worked in the industry for a couple of years. And then, on September 11, 2001, the world changed. The United States was under attack and New York City was the first target. I can remember nearly every detail of that day. My friend Tiiu and I were freelancing and had an early meeting before we had to be at work in Midtown. We jumped on the No. 6 subway and, fortunately, got off at 8:45 a.m., one minute before hijacked American Airlines Flight 11 hit the first tower. I always think about how lucky we were. Had we taken the next subway we would have been trapped underground for God knows how many hours.

Off we went to *what we thought* was just another typical day in New York City. It was a little hazy and hot, but September in the city usually is. The art deco building we worked in had a small elevator and we headed to the third floor. The studio was still quiet, and the day was about to begin. It was approximately 9 a.m.

My cell phone rings. It's my mom. "Are you OK?

"Of course. What's going on?" I ask, thinking it's a little weird she's calling.

"An airplane hit the World Trade Center and it's all over the news!"

I rush to the nearest window and look outside. It's eerily quiet.

"No—nothing here. Everything seems fine."

I shout out to the studio, "Anyone hear about a plane crashing into the World Trade Center?"

One of my co-workers pulls up something on his computer screen and we gather around. Hearing the turbulence that I've now created in the office, the company president came out and said, very nonchalantly, "Oh, I saw that. It was a small plane—nothing to worry about."

We got the cue to go back to work. But my phone continued to ring. The next call was my friend's mom from Galveston.

"Melanie, can you please go check on Ari? I can't get in touch with her. She's probably at Lenox Hill Hospital waiting for the ambulances." Ari, a nurse practitioner and one of my earliest childhood friends—practically a sister to me—lived a few blocks from where I was working. I promised to check in on her as the day progressed.

I went back to the small corner window where I had stood minutes earlier. We just learned that the South Tower had been hit. I spotted lines of smoke in the not-too-far distance. I heard a few sirens, but the streets were still quiet. No fire trucks. No ambulances. When I finally spoke to Ari, she told me that all the hospitals were waiting, and waiting, and waiting for an onslaught of patients that never came. There were very few survivors.

We had no idea what was going on. No idea that we were in the middle of what was to become the deadliest attack ever on U.S. soil. Two thousand, seven hundred and fifty-three souls were lost seven miles south of where I was standing.

My brother was now calling. He was home watching the apocalyptic day unfold. He wanted to know why I was still at work.

"The entire nation is at home watching this, Melanie! Why are you still at your office?"

I can honestly say we were in a time warp that day. Leadership decided it would be better for us to work through the fire. If we lived outside the city, we could leave early.

Looking back, I call bullshit. It was obnoxious and absurd to think that "working through it" was helping any of us. Nobody could focus! Deadlines didn't matter if our clients were dead! Screw that! What about our friends and family who worked downtown? Where are they? How are they? Are they even alive?

I looked out another window that faced the Queensboro Bridge. It was cataclysmic. I was in utter shock by what I saw—hundreds of thousands of people leaving Manhattan by foot. The 59th Street

Bridge was one of the only ways to leave. I went straight into panic mode.

Shock and awe led me to visions of the Y2K commercial blitz with elephants and giraffes and wild beasts running rampant in the streets. I headed outside to find a sky full of gray haze. It was mid-afternoon, but it looked like dusk. Bits and pieces of debris floated past me as I sat bewildered on a white polypropylene sofa bench outside the Conrad Shop.

To this day, I can smell the rancid smoke and feel the torn hearts in the streets.

The following months were dark with sadness. The city, in a way, froze. Fall turned to winter and New York kept getting colder, physically and emotionally. I looked for another job to get me out of the doldrums, but there were few opportunities. I could have worked in Connecticut and commuted three hours each day, but I opted out.

I was at a fork in the road. Do I stay in New York and work through the pain, or pack my bags and head back to Texas to be closer to my family? It was May 21, 2002. In hindsight, this date—my birthday—would become very fortuitous many years later. I was celebrating my 29th birthday with singleton friends at a tapas restaurant in Soho. We sipped sangria as music played. Halfway through the meal, I heard that familiar inner voice: "Melanie, it's time to go back to Texas." My butterflies came back, and I knew what to do.

A month later I returned to Houston—this time for good.

I am still unclear if, in the five years I was gone, the city of Houston grew up or I did. Everything felt different. I think it was a little bit of both. I learned to love my newfangled city of residence. I found another group of friends, and I grew in my career as an interior designer.

Fun and laughter and squeezing everything beautiful out of life—not marriage—became my priority. When I finally settled down in my mid-thirties, I began to realize that my dream of building a family would be challenging. My age was catching up with me and I would have to look at alternative methods to grow my family.

02

I Always Knew It

From the time I was a teenager, I somehow knew I would adopt.

I don't know when it started, but the idea already was in my head when scandal surfaced in the halls of Ball High School, usually outside the cosmetology classroom. Strollers being pushed through the hallway were not necessarily common, but they were definitely talking points for classroom chatter. And we did a lot of that.

Between classes we'd discuss what we'd do in that kind of "situation," and would often offer advice—ridiculous high school advice that involved medically questionable rituals—about how to avoid or fix it.

"I'd take a boiling hot bath and soak in it for hours" one of my friends would confidently say.

And that was one of the less ridiculous solutions some of us came up with.

The idea of someone anywhere near my age being pregnant was foreign to me. Unthinkable, even. My parents would have killed me first, so it wouldn't have mattered.

Some girls romanticized the idea of pregnancy and talked about maternity clothes and rushing to the hospital. Others were disgusted by it, disgusted at the thought of a creature growing inside their belly. Or of their belly expanding to fit another life.

Me, I took it in stride. Because I knew it would never be me. Maybe in some weird subconscious way I was either creating my future or seeing how it would unfold and preparing for it from a young age. For some reason I was obsessed with Chinese adoption. It must have been the growing trend during the '80s and '90s. China, China, China was all I could think. Of course, I had never been there.

Not until I was in my early thirties, single and wanting to travel to far and exotic places, did I get to the Far East. In the summer of 2005, my cousin Bret and I visited one of my oldest and dearest friends, Aly, who had been living in China for the past 10 years. We started in Shanghai and then traveled to meet her in Beijing. Aly helped us wind our way through the ancient city and into Inner Mongolia. I loved every minute of the journey, even staying in an old Russian insane asylum that had been converted to what locals claim was one of the nicest hotels in the area. It was disgusting.

Aly and I had a long-running joke that she could pick up a couple of Chinese babies when I was ready. She had spent quite a bit of time in the countryside and had, at that point, become integrated into Chinese culture. Bret even got in on the joke with an occasional laugh and chuckle.

It was a great trip, and for the next few weeks I basked in the fun memories. Then September 2005 hit. Hurricane Rita began to threaten our area. Houston and Galveston residents were going crazy on the heels of Hurricane Katrina that had just devastated New Orleans. The sky was going to fall.

Fearing the worst, I caravanned with my family to San Antonio in the most horrific traffic jam I have ever witnessed. We were stuck on Interstate Highway 10, basically at a standstill with what seemed like the rest of Houston. My father would sporadically walk beside the car, smoking his cigar while I drove, inching along at 2 or 3 miles per hour. My brother and sister-in-law were a few cars behind with their two young children and a third due at any moment. We were all concerned that Rachael might deliver along the road. *Oy*. Pure drama.

The drive from Houston to San Antonio usually takes three hours. Four with traffic. That day, it took 12 hours. When we finally got to the Alamo, my parents, their two dogs, my new puppy, and I tumbled out of the car. Finally!

We spent the next couple of days at the Menger Hotel, where I exhausted my mental energy thinking how amazing this historic hotel could look after a nice renovation. It's a habit I've picked up as a commercial interior designer. I'm accustomed to walking into spaces and dissecting them bit by bit. Needless to say, it kept me distracted during this extremely emotional upheaval.

Friends and family from around the country were calling to check on us. My dad was constantly on his phone—we joked that he had a direct line to FEMA. Fortunately, the entire experience ended up being unnecessary. Hurricane Rita, though a monster storm, ended up sparing Houston and Galveston.

I was ready to get back home. On the journey, some friends called to let me know that a bunch of them would be meeting at El Tiempo, a Mexican restaurant off Washington Avenue. It was one of the only places open after the "storm" that actually had food and drinks.

The car couldn't get there fast enough for me. I think we were still driving when I hopped out.

"Bye, Mom and Dad -- see you later!"

I ran as fast as possible to our table of about 20 people.

After decompressing with a margarita from an extremely stressful weekend—back with friends in our city now safe from hurricane danger, Chris and I connected romantically for the first time. I told him about our future together– that we were going to marry and adopt a Chinese baby. He had no idea what he was signing up for and gladly admits it to this very day.

Looking back at the events where my family was forced to evacuate, what could have been an unfortunate episode turned into something miraculously wonderful. If it hadn't been for the hurricane (that never hit Houston or Galveston), maybe Chris and I wouldn't have ended up hanging out that fortuitous night.

After that, our paths were destined to be together. Chris and I married a year and ten months later. I would have jumped right into the wedding dress, but my husband-to-be had a "stupid" four-season rule—we had to be together for a full year and go through each month to see how we would fare with each other. I would constantly roll my eyes. I was 32 and ready. He was 40 and had no idea. I'll admit, in hindsight, there was wisdom there.

Down we march to our wedding, on October 27th, 2007. I had already stopped taking both birth control and Prozac, which I had been on since I was 18 years old. Some people might think of depression as a dark little secret, but it has been the catalyst for who I am today. Sad and Anxious, meet Happy and Whimsical. The two sides of my personality go hand-in-hand.

Mistake No. 1: Chris was not aware that I had stopped taking birth control.

Mistake No. 2: Stopping Prozac was a terrible idea. I was feeling good and did not want to be on meds while pregnant—which I innocently thought would happen quickly after our wedding.

That first year was extremely difficult. I wanted to get pregnant so badly that I risked my mental health, and that, in turn, rocked our marriage.

I was beyond unhappy. I was brutally sad. And frustrated.

And angry.

I felt stuck and I didn't know how to change my life circumstances. I felt everyone's eyes on me looking for the signs of an expectant mother-to-be. Chris didn't care because at that point, he was happy with just the two of us. He also wasn't aware that I had taken myself off my medication, but when I eventually revealed the situation, he was livid.

"Get back on your damn meds, Melanie!

You are not yourself anymore!"

And that's what I did, for Chris—and me and my sanity.

It's funny: I say I wanted to get pregnant so badly, but the truth is, I've never *really* wanted to *be* pregnant. In fact, the idea has always sort of scared me. I've struggled my entire life with body image and have been fearful of what would happen to my short, stocky body with a baby inside. I also don't like anything associated with pain and discomfort, both inherent with the fertility process in women. All that aside, I still tried to get pregnant because that was the natural order of life, right?

I wasn't too concerned the first couple of years. After all, we were newlyweds and sharing a new life together. I had waited my entire life to find my soulmate—of course, this Southern Jewish girl never in a million years dreamed he would come as a short, stocky, middle-aged, graphic designer named Chris (*not Jewish*). But he did. And I fell in love with him and his spirit.

I went to the doctor for my annual check-up and waited to hear the words he'd so often said in the past, "You have a *beautiful* uterus!"

To my chagrin, those words did not come through during this particular visit. Earlier I had mentioned that we were trying to get pregnant. The doctor looked at me in a sad but caring way and handed me a card for a fertility specialist. I was underwhelmed. Actually, I was angry and in disbelief. A year later I switched doctors to a woman who came highly recommended by friends. She said that due to my age and the amount of time it had taken us to get pregnant, I should consider alternatives. This time, I actually heard the message.

I decided to keep my options open, so I made an appointment with the specialist she recommended. I walked into the waiting room—which (if you'll excuse the interior designer in me) was very nice. There was a flowing water feature, a large fish tank that was supposed to be a calming influence, and a sea of soft seating. On the walls were baby after baby after baby picture, hung as trophies to show how amazing this group was in helping people have their offspring.

I wanted to vomit as I thought to myself, "Seriously? Has it come to this?"

I met the doctor alone for a consultation. He was tall, attractive with light blond hair and a thin build. He sat me at his desk, and we started talking statistics. First thing was a chart he pulled up on screen showing how, at my age—which was about 37 at this point—the probability of becoming pregnant was statistically getting more unlikely with each passing day. What I heard was him selling his life-altering, steroid-injecting, blah blah blah for about an hour. Chris was on the speaker phone listening to all of this from his office.

Then it was time to read Chris's fortune—very unfortunate as well. Chris had done some "homework" in preparation for the visit. The doctor discussed his sperm count and claimed that it was lower than average—quite a bit, in fact.

OK, so maybe the problem wasn't me.

Maybe it was Chris. Or maybe it was both of us as a team. Go Team!

I later came to find out that my brilliant husband delivered his first homework assignment in a plastic Ziploc that he leisurely took over in a brown paper bag. Gross.

By this point, I had already made the decision that we were O-U-T of the baby-making game. For many families the fertility specialist was a godsend. But I did not need them for us to have a family. Adoption came back to my senses.

Game on!

03

Tougher Than We Thought

The December holidays are a big event for our Promecene household. Growing up, the biggest gifts came December 25th. The little ones like socks and trinkets were for Hanukkah. With the merging of our big Jewish and Catholic families, Christmas Eve (which we now call "Chrismakkah") became a time for everyone to celebrate. Christmas Eve 2006 was particularly special: It's when Chris and I announced our engagement. I think of that moment with smiles and warmth. The children in our respective families were young (and there were lots of them—13 total). Everybody sang and danced and ate. It was like the celebration at the end of *How the Grinch Stole Christmas,* and we were the *Whos* in *Who*-ville.

It was only natural we'd choose this season several years later for another wonderful announcement.

Everyone was gathered in the living room of our house on Queensloch Drive. Chris clinked his glass and started to make a toast before the grand opening of overflowing stocking stuffers. And I started to talk.

"We have another announcement to make. Chris and I are going to start the adoption process!"

For couples like us, this announcement is the equivalent of declaring yourself pregnant. Little did we know that we'd be pregnant for more than three years.

I was super excited and everyone else was, too. It was a wonderful and scary moment.

"We're thinking about international adoption—China," I say in one breath.

The onslaught of questions began, but I had no answers. I just knew that I felt much better this year than I had every other past Christmas Eve hoping but unable to announce that I was pregnant. Now I had control. And I wanted a Chinese baby!

In hindsight, I was a little naïve. I had a preconceived idea of a baby from China, and I couldn't see around it. I just figured things would fall into place now that the wheels were in motion. If I wasn't going to be pregnant, then I'd adopt from China, just like Aly and I had joked about years earlier. The idea of a baby from Korea or Russia or Texas never entered my mind.

The next day was just as emotional, if not more. I put the idea out into the world. Now I had to start the research process. My father, never afraid to voice his opinion, asked "Why China?"

I had no response. It was my brother who stepped up to answer in my absence.

"She's always wanted this and has been talking about it since high school." I do not think my dad was aware of that, or the fact that I had wanted to adopt as a child.

I had been up the night before researching Chinese adoption. I knew it would be complex and take many years. Two years was the general timeframe. I took a deep breath and braced myself for the ride.

We were at my folks' condo for brunch and all I could do was cry. I was an emotional wreck. If I had been pregnant, people would have said it was my hormones. The only explanation I had was my tendency to cry *a lot*—when I'm happy, when I'm sad, mad, or anxious. Now I was the latter. And the tears kept coming. My family was not quite sure what to do with me. I was a mess. As "fixers," they wanted to make everything better for me. Easier. My brother's best friend from college had recently adopted, so Kenny called Travis. "Can you talk with her?"

And that was the kickoff.

Travis was very kind and soft-spoken. My brother had told him that I wanted to go through an international adoption. Travis advised, "If nothing else, talk to Louise, our adoption consultant. She is very kind and be able to guide you."

Up until that point I had no idea there were adoption consultants. I eventually came to learn that there was an entire Adoption Industrial Complex of consultants and placement agencies—some, of course, better than others.

Chris and I followed Travis's lead and had an initial consultation with Louise a couple of weeks later. As I closed the door to the car behind me and glanced at Louise's house, I tried to absorb the moment, "Here we go," I told myself. "Deep breath, Melanie."

In retrospect, I was entirely unprepared for the ups and downs that would rock our lives for the next few years.

We rang the doorbell and a smiling woman in her mid-60s opened the door. She welcomed us into her living room, and we all sat down. It was a nice two-story house. She had framed pictures of her children on the dark wood side tables, I'm guessing they were adults at this point.

This was basically a get-to-know each other session. As Chris and I explained our desire to adopt internationally, she remained stoic.

"There are many challenges with adoption, and these become compounded when dealing internationally," she said. She went on to discuss various countries and obstacles within each; which were "easier", and which were no longer available—like Russia.

She continued, "The good thing about adoption is that you will get a baby in the end. The bad thing is that it can take a while." She talked about different agencies and options, but I was not interested. My focus was China.

Adoption in China has been problematic for many. As one of the most populated nations on earth, there is an abundance of neglected children, and a majority end up in orphanages—which are dismal. Many times, babies are left on their own without much interaction. Many of these infants suffer from some abnormality or dysfunction; healthy babies are rare. Even so, the government prefers that Chinese adopt Chinese. Americans who are looking to expand their families through international adoption are typically a second-to-last resort.

With that said, Louise wanted us to get what we wanted. We ended the conversation, took her tidbits of wisdom and left with much food for thought.

We had just verbally downloaded our history—opening up our souls and genetics for this woman (whom we just met) to tabulate and figure out our best adoptive course. She would call us within the week after consulting with others. I remained positive and hopeful. Very hopeful!

I received a call later that week. Louise laid out the pros and cons. I had a history of depression which, at that time, was typically a disqualifier due to China's medication restrictions. Chris was in his mid-to-late 40s—not good if you're comparing our stats to a spry young Chinese couple. We could pay a lot of money, wait in the long line and "hopefully" get a baby down the road, but there was no guarantee. We probably would be rejected due to my genetic history with depression. However, there was a *small* probability that we could get a baby if we were open to one with birth defects including, but not limited to facial distortions, abnormal limbs, hearing damage, and the like. The chances, however, were still relatively low.

Bust.

I was devastated. I knew it would be hard, but I did not think that I would basically be blackballed by the Chinese government. "I fucking hate them!" I screamed in the phone, with tears running down my face.

"Would you want to consider Korea? The process is easier in that country. There's also Latin America and Africa," Louise said.

The answer was a firm "No." I closed the door to the international process very quickly.

I hung up the phone, called Chris, and cried. I mean *really* cried. I had to take a break, catch my breath and wrap my head around the fact that my childhood dream would not be realized.

So, take a break I did. Mental survival kicked in and I slowly distanced myself from the grief and anger. It took a few months before I could consider alternatives.

Then I was ready. Plan B. Where do we go from here?

1
2
3

04

Open, Semi-Open, Closed & Confusing

Chris and I returned to Louise, this time understanding that China was out, which my family was relieved about. They had been concerned about the difficulties we would have to endure with a child who needed so much medical attention.

We're back on Louise's sofa, and I'm sinking into the cushion. It's super *cush.*

"I've put together a list of agencies around Texas that I think would fit your needs well. You will need to interview them and get a feel for how they work. The good news is that we live in one of the best states to adopt."

Until that point, I was unaware about Texas adoption laws, or any laws or regulations regarding adoption. I knew very little about the process, except that it could take a long time, whatever that meant.

However, in that moment, I was happy to learn that Texas laws were very pro-adoptive parent.

"At least that's one good thing," I told myself.

Not knowing what type of agency we were looking for, or even that agency options existed, Chris and I listened as Louise described the various types of adoption: Semi-Open, Fully Open, and Closed. The agency you are drawn to depends on the sort of openness you are looking for.

Louise explained that Semi-Open involves one or two face-to-face meetings with the birth parents before delivery and/or at placement. Pictures and letters are shared through the agency for up to 18 years.

With Fully Open adoption, the adoptive family and birth parents disclose all identifying information. Direct communication occurs through phone calls, emails, and text messages. Face-to-face meetings with the birth parents take place before and after the birth, for as long as (and to the degree that) both parties feel comfortable.

Closed adoption embraces confidentiality at the highest level. There is no communication between the birth parents and adoptive parents.

Based on the information presented, Chris and I agreed that closed adoption was not for us. However, we were still unsure whether we preferred semi-open or fully open. "What's the difference again? Why is one better than the other?" I asked.

Louise said she believed fully open adoption was the healthiest for the baby over time. However, it would be our decision and we, as parents, would need to make the final determination.

"You'll need to visit the agencies and get a feeling for how they operate and work with both birth mothers and adoptive parents. Don't forget to ask about their delivery rate—how many children were adopted over the past few years. They should have a list to share with you. Each agency also has different requirements."

Louise then handed us a list of agencies, fees, stats, and articles pulled nicely together into one concise bible (a 3-ring binder).

"I selected these agencies because they were also open to working with dual-religion couples. It may become a little more challenging being Jewish. You see, many birth moms want to place their baby in a family system they can relate to and understand. Most birth mothers are Christian and want their child to grow up with Christmas and Easter."

In the back of my mind I thought to myself, "First we had to deal with xenophobia, then ageism, then mental health, and now religion?"

I felt whacked by discrimination on multiple fronts, but the religious thing hit my core. I've always considered myself much more spiritual than ritual but Judaism is so much a part of who I am. It's my heritage, my value system. I understand philosophically that religion is a preference. However, it saddens me to think in our modern age we still have to contend with this type of religious undercurrent.

Growing up in a smallish town with only a handful of other Jewish kids, we kinda felt like a special club. We'd take off a couple of days of school during the fall High Holy days to attend religious services—but would hang out in the bathroom chatting half the time, usually during the rabbi's sermon. Classmates were intrigued and would ask what we did. We Jewish kids were an anomaly. A definite outlier, but one of the good kinds. My childhood friends still talk about the fun they had when my mom would visit our elementary school and tell the story of Hanukkah, make potato pancakes and play dreidel. Funny how those memories stick.

Although I ended up marrying a man outside of my faith, our marriage works because we appreciate each other's backgrounds. We came to an agreement before marriage that if we had children, they would grow up Jewish. Chris was not a practicing Catholic and as long as we could continue to celebrate the holidays that he grew up treasuring, like Christmas and Easter (without church—just presents and egg hunts and family gatherings), there would be no issues. And that seemed like a win to me. This was the first time in our marriage where religion actually became an issue—as we were trying to adopt. My core was angry and my heart was sad.

I'm not sure if the religious issue Louise brought up, or any of the other issues at hand, had the same effect on Chris, but I could tell he was getting flustered. After listening to the monetary formalities and hurdles, Chris blurted out half-heartedly, "Can't we just buy a baby?"

Louise did not laugh. I'm not sure what she thought, but it wasn't good.

At that moment, Louise transitioned from consultant to authority. We hired her to help us through the adoption process, and we quickly realized we would also need to navigate our relationship with her. We knew Kind Louise from the first time we met her. Her gentle nature and desire to help us made that clear. We got to know Firm Louise, as well, when she instructed us that there were no shortcuts in adoption—that regulations had to be followed. As our conversations progressed, we began treading new waters—and Disapproving Louise manifested. Chris and I kept our emotions in check by falling back on humor, but we realized Louise did not "get" our sense of humor, which ended up making us feel worse.

She took on a very serious tone and began describing the sequence by which agencies took care of the birth mothers and the stringent guidelines placed on the industry. It was an awkward moment, but we plowed on.

Louise thoughtfully pulled together a package of pros and cons of the three agencies we should consider. One was in San Antonio, one in Austin, and one in Fort Worth. We knew the most about the agency in Fort Worth. Almost every person I talked to knew about it as well. It was one of the oldest agencies in Texas, with origins dating back to the 1880s. Back then, it focused on locating homes for orphans. It has since evolved into lobbying international adoptions, counseling, maternity services, education, and philanthropy.

Most of the people I spoke with had good experiences with that agency, but for some reason I did not want to use it. It was a gut instinct, maybe one of my strongest. Had I chosen this particular agency; I would not have ended up with the whirlwind of experiences which eventually led me to my beautiful child.

There was an adoption education session that was approaching in a couple of weeks, sponsored by the agency in Austin. Louise encouraged us to attend this group session so we could get a better understanding of open adoption and learn about the agency. As a bonus, if we liked this group and decided to go with that agency, attending the weekend retreat would provide us with their 10 hours of educational requirements and get us on track to working through the first stages of the adoption process.

We signed up immediately.

There were agency adoption education requirements—two hours per quarter, to be exact. This can be done through parenting classes, watching videos, or even reading books or magazines. In hindsight, I had no idea the amount of "education" I would be receiving, which was a *lot* over a *long* period of time.

We decided to visit the agency in San Antonio on the way to Austin. We piggybacked a night, staying with Chris's brother, Will, and family in San Antonio. It was kind of nice to take a long weekend.

We met with the San Antonio agency Friday afternoon and were very impressed. We liked the director a lot. She was warm and kind and gave us some adoption books to look through. The agency was based in a little house that resembled a lovely cottage, sweet and picturesque—what I envisioned an adoption agency would be. By the time we left the agency, Chris and I agreed that we were very comfortable with this group and it could be the right fit for us.

We would probably have signed that day if we had not already committed to the second agency visit. It was here where I learned the importance of visiting different agencies and talking with multiple people to better understand their experiences, perspectives, and insights. Every agency has its own way of doing things, from payment options to homework requirements all the way to communication with the birth mother after the child is born.

By the time we went back for drinks at Chris's brother's house, we were relaxed and happy. I remember lying on the bed with my sister-in-law Angela and going through the motions of the day, step by step. It was a nice experience. I didn't think I really needed to go to Austin the next day, but the sun rose and off we went.

The 90-minute drive Saturday morning went quickly. We pulled into an office building that was new and modern—completely different from the little cottage we visited the day before. The group hosting the seminar appeared very professional. There were

13 people in our group, including the facilitators. It's hard to remember, but I think there were five couples and a single woman, probably in her late 30s. I saw myself in her at one point in my life, before Chris.

The agency had two facilitators who walked us through the day's events. We talked about everything from misconceptions about adoption to why we were there and going through the process ourselves. The day was long, but the hours went fast. It was sobering to hear some of the people in our group discuss their journeys. Some had children and others didn't. It was probably a combination of couples in their late 20s and 30s. Everyone was very nice and supportive.

Each person in the group ended up sharing at some point during the day. The good thing was that I was used to these types of group counseling sessions from both personal and professional experience. Chris, on the other hand, had a very eye-opening experience. I think this was the first time he had taken part in an intimate group session where you share some of your most personal thoughts with total strangers.

Although it was frustrating to sit through classes where we had to learn about child development, I also found it energizing to be there. It was the first step in our process with an actual agency and was enlightening.

The morning flowed into afternoon, and a panel of birth mothers joined our session at the end of the day. There might have been five women who, individually, had very different journeys. Some birth mothers were very talkative; others remained quiet.

There was one birth mother who sat in silence and looked at the floor the entire hour. She was probably around nine months pregnant and looked as if she could pop at any moment. She had long dark hair and sorrowful blue eyes. Pain was strewn across her face. My heart ached for her.

What struck me the most was how connected each of these birth mothers was to the child she birthed. These women brought pictures, some in boxes and others in albums, and were happy to share the importance of the relationship with their adoptive families. It brought them peace to know that their babies were with families they selected and who would provide better lives for the children they birthed. There was no animosity or resentment—just love for their adoptive families.

I knew almost nothing about open adoption before that day, but by the end of our group session I was determined to have nothing but a fully open adoption. That session opened my eyes and I learned that a fully open adoption is the healthiest way to let your child know where he or she came from—that giving a child to another couple was difficult and done purely out of love.

I determined at that moment that if I was fortunate enough to one day adopt a child, I would make sure my son or daughter respected his or her birth mother for her altruism. Now that I am a mother, I am letting my son know, as he grows, that he was born out of love, and that his birth mother has a special place in our hearts. My hope is that he will only have respect for her and the decisions she made to carry and deliver him to us.

After we finished the day's session, Chris and I headed to our hotel off South Congress and were ready to hit the bar. That was a poor decision. The bar was at the swanky rooftop pool. We sat with our gin and tonics, watching young, tan, beautiful people enjoying themselves, and decided to go right back to our room. It was only 5 p.m. Neither Chris nor I had the energy to go out for dinner, so we ordered room service. While we sat and waited for our food to arrive, I had a very long crying session. I was haunted by the image of the pregnant woman with long black hair and blue eyes, looking down at the floor in silence. What was she thinking? What did she think of us?

Was she the circus act—or were we? I was mentally and physically exhausted. Chris was, too. We ate dinner in bed, silent, watching some movie on TV, and falling asleep soon afterward. It couldn't have been later than 8 p.m.

The next day we rose and headed back to the office building for our final round-table discussion. Everyone in our group seemed a little looser and a tad friendlier than the day before. There were adoption books on the tables, and some were being passed around. I had not paid much attention to them before, but as they were now in front of me, I tried to focus. But I couldn't. I was too emotionally drained.

We met with the agency director and I immediately felt like this was the place for us. I thought to myself, "if they can orchestrate such a well-organized, thoughtful program then I am in."

And that was that. We signed up, I think that day—or at least that week. The paperwork had begun.

05

Under the Microscope

Any great growth spurt can be painful. That applies to physical growth, spiritual growth, and even the growth of a family. Some of my pain involved my own insecurities—which I had to shed (or at least put aside for a while) in my quest to become a parent. And nothing nourishes insecurity like a Professional Evaluator in your home.

Yes, an "evaluator" actually came to our house to review and critique our home environment—and us. The technical term is "home study," and it's where a social worker visits a house to ensure prospective parents are who they say they are. The State of Texas required us to have one comprehensive home study, but these studies have an expiration date. After one year, they're no longer considered valid. Because it took so long for us to find our son, we had to update our study. And then update it again.

Our home study was performed by a licensed social worker so the government could be assured that we were fit to be parents. In my mind, that was a giant crock of shit. Seriously, most any adolescent girl or half-baked woman can get pregnant without being emotionally, spiritually, or physically equipped to handle a child. But as adoptive parents—grown people who want a family but are prevented by biology from having a child the conventional way—we had to have our lives picked apart and our homes inspected by a social worker? It felt like a jab. An extremely frustrating one. It was not fair.

But hey, life's not always fair. Chris and I understood the rules—or at least we learned to live with them as the process churned. We didn't always like the rules, but we played by them.

Intellectually, I understand that the state needs to ensure that potential adoptive parents are fit to raise children. I agree that someone needed to check to see that we were not serial killers, pedophiles, or just all-around bad dudes. But on a personal level, I felt like I was enduring an endless series of Judging Sessions. Was I saying the right thing? Was my house good enough? Clean enough? Big enough? The list went on and on, at least it in my head, and I didn't just second-guess myself. I third-guessed everything I said and fourth-guessed everything I did.

I had heard stories through the Adoptive Parent Rumor Mill that some social workers would rifle through sock and undie drawers to see how organized potential parents were. In preparation for this, my mom—the Organizer Extraordinaire—helped me get my house in top order. We stripped the closets and color-coded nearly anything that could be coded. I was prepared! Fortunately, Louise did not snoop through our socks. She went through our house very respectfully, noting the required smoke detectors and any possible hazards, always the professional. She never even opened a closet door. But if she had, boy would she have been impressed.

Chris and I were assessed prior to our baby's arrival three times—one home study and two updates. After birth, we had five post-placement visits, one per month. During the sixth month we went to court to make the adoption official. But I'm getting ahead of myself.

Louise had a dual role. She was both our social worker (whom we paid) and a gatekeeper with our agency (which we paid). You might be asking yourself, "Isn't it a bit weird that we're paying her to critique us and give the results to our agency … which we're *also* paying?"

The answer—to us, at least—is yes. It *is* weird. This was the toughest thing for my husband to swallow.

On top of that, we seemed to be paying out of pocket at every turn. Although we always will be grateful to Louise for her guidance and her support, we still had to hire her to check a box that says we're

"OK to parent" for our agency (which we're paying about $40,000, and which *engages Louise*).

And this is not considered baby buying? Of course not, silly! It's just another part of *the process*.

06

Accentuate the Positive

When Chris and I decided to adopt, we anticipated bureaucracy.

But arts and crafts? That didn't enter our thinking.

And it was a huge undertaking.

Part of the adoption process is creating an "adoption profile" book. It's just like it says—a profile of us but instead of being on internet sites like Match or LinkedIn, this was an actual book—a hardcover product that we created for birth parents to leaf through during their agency visits. Some of the books we first reviewed were pretty old-school, patchwork like. They must have been done quite a few years beforehand. I could see and feel the energy input from each photo that was cut and pasted on the paper alongside construction paper hearts and flowers. Pretty sweet, huh? But that was not us. Good thing I married a graphic designer who took this matter into his own hands.

Our job was to curate something that would reflect our values and talk about who we were as a couple but didn't reflect our lives *too* accurately. Just like in today's world of social media, there's etiquette. There's real life and then there's the life portrayed on social media.

Our profile book was designed sort of like Tinder for adoption. Our job wasn't to accurately reflect ourselves, but to market ourselves. We had to craft a version of Mel and Chris that would appeal to birth parents who were much younger than we were, who came from different backgrounds, and may or may not be educated. It was tricky. Although Chris was a master with Photoshop and crafting a carefully curated profile, we still had quite a project on our hands.

Chris quickly created our profiles to get the wheels in motion. He started with pictures of us together and then built sections for us individually—our lifestyle, likes, favorite things, family, pets, etc. It was really a very narcissistic undertaking and, basically, a marketing ploy. How best could we sell ourselves to prospective parents? How could we show our life and essence in a few pages?

Chris did a brilliant job at capturing everyday moments in our photos. Some of our pictures were nothing special—us lounging on the sofa or relaxing on the beach with family. It was amazing how a little Photoshop editing could enhance menial daily tasks and activities. To me, Chris's editing wizardry was magic.

My brilliant husband edited the pages with a storytelling mindset: what was the best way for us to showcase who we were individually and as a couple? What kind of parents would we be? We included a little verbiage to help explain events and people. We had friends and family look at our profile book for perspective and feedback. True critiquing.

Although Chris did a great job putting the book together, he compiled it very quickly, and it needed massaging. As a graphic artist, he took this negatively at times but understood that it was not about what we liked. It was about the sell. And yes, at that point we were in the sales business.

I was warned against putting anything "too Jewish" in the book, but those warnings were couched in anodyne language. Basically, I was being told to hide my religion. Christmas trees were OK, but menorahs were not. It was frequently conveyed that birth parents needed to relate to something about us—and the pros told me a menorah was typically not that.

Just to be clear, not all agencies have this bias, especially ones that are geared toward certain faith traditions.

I was in a bit of shock followed by a tinge of anger. Seriously, what were the rules? I could show a photo of a Shabbat with candles because that appeared to be a normal candlelit meal, but not a menorah. I had to pretend not to be Jewish. I'm sure they'd argue that was not what they meant to imply, but for the time we were orchestrating our profile book, that's what it felt like.

Keeping that in mind, we limited the Jewish stuff to our wedding photo with our entire family under the chuppah. We made a special point to take a few selfies in front of European churches during our travels. We also added a family photo from one of our weekly Sunday family dinners—right in front of my sister-in-law's wall of crucifixes.

I struggled with the thought of not telling the whole truth, but as time progressed, Chris and I learned to trust our instincts. After all, our book was about us, and we realized there were no bad moves as long as they came from our heart.

So, our book was getting juiced up with lots of pictures, events, life scenes, family, friends and pets. We said a few things about the photos and kept the message short and simple as our rule of thumb. Long paragraphs did not translate well. We had to remember that what we were creating was called a book, but it really was more like a magazine. Which version were we? *Architectural Digest*? *House & Garden*? *Southern Living*? Definitely no. I think Chris and I ended up being a little on the *Dwell* magazine artsy-fartsy side.

For me, the hardest part of our profile book was writing a letter to our future birth mother. This took me quite a bit of time to write.

Actually, it took a tremendously long time—with multiple rewrites. I think I went through about 10 drafts before my first full-page letter was ready. My little trash can was overflowing with balled-up sheets of lined yellow paper. I realized my initial letters were too long, wordy and overly complicated.

I finally condensed my love letter to a few short paragraphs and tried to be authentically me. My highest priority was to be pure in my thoughts and wishes—for both the birth parents and baby. I knew they would hold on to this book forever. The words needed to be perfect, and for me they finally flowed:

Dear Birth Mother,

Welcome to our book! We are Melanie and Chris Promecene from Houston, Texas, and have been married for five years (seven at this point). We are reaching out to you in hopes that you might be able to answer our prayer to grow our family through adoption.

We understand the decision to place your child for adoption is one of the hardest yet most loving, unselfish things a person can do. With that in mind we are writing to you with an open heart and loving spirit.

Should you select us as adoptive parents, we want you to know that you will always be held in the highest regard and our child will know that he or she came from a very loving and caring individual. If you choose, we are open to having an ongoing relationship with you. We promise to encourage and support our child emotionally, spiritually, and intellectually, honoring his or her unique qualities and heritage. As parents, we will do everything in our power to provide a beautiful life for our child.

With love and admiration,

Melanie and Chris

During our introductory group session in Austin, we were told that many times the birth mother would know you're her "pick" just from the photo on the cover. It might be your eyes or something you're wearing. In our case, our birth mother liked my smile. She pulled our book and put it to the side without opening it, reviewed the others, and came back to us.

I'm glad it was my smile. Our picture was taken on a street in Florence. I had just come from the flea market and was wearing a new hat, one of my signature statements. I still do not know why Chris selected that particular photo for our cover, but I am delighted he did.

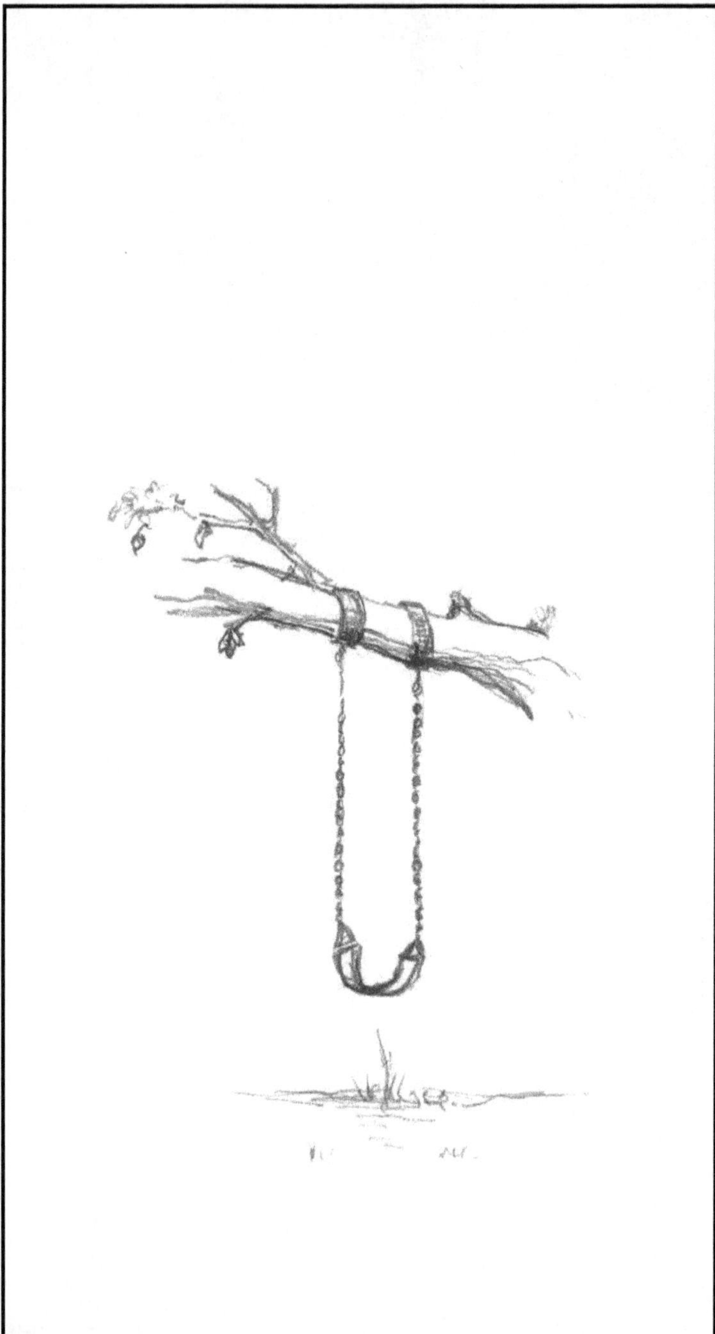

07

Labor(less) Pains

We were prepared for a lot of the difficulties that sprang up, but to paraphrase Tom Petty, the way-yay-ting was the hardest part.

By a whole lot.

We waited and waited. A month passed, and no adoption. Then two. Then four. Then a year.

It took so long, in fact, that our home study expired, and we had to have a second one. And then a third!

It was as if I was pregnant for 1,040 days—always wondering when it would be "time."

In case you're thinking, 'two-and-a-half years? Forget it,' I have some advice: Don't worry. You'll get through it. I know because I did.

Part of the reason it took so long for us to find the right child, and for the right child to find us, is that we had a detailed list of the characteristics we required in birth parents and in babies. I hadn't thought about that when I decided to adopt, but as Chris and I talked about it, we realized we had to develop parameters. And we had to stick with them, no matter how painful it might sometimes be—as we would learn later on. Soon after we chose our agency, we spent hours thinking about factors that had never even entered our consciousness. The agency gave us a questionnaire that helped us develop those parameters. What were we willing to accept? How much could we overlook? Oddly enough, we didn't think about things like race, ethnicity, gender, or socioeconomic status. Instead, we looked at drugs, alcohol, and genetic histories.

It was more complicated and difficult than we realized. And even when we made firm decisions based on what we were convinced was solid reasoning, complications kept arising. We learned that most of the time, there is a reason birth parents place babies for adoption. If they had support and funding behind them, they would most likely keep the child. *We* had to consider *their* challenging situations and extenuating circumstances.

We decided we would accept a child of a different race than us and that we had no specific gender in mind. We had to decide if we would accept a child whose birth mother had used drugs, which was not as black and white. There were so many elements to consider, and if we hadn't had such a specific set of requirements, our wait probably would have been shorter. And without those requirements, Noah would not be our son today.

Our wait was longer than most. According to a 2015-2016 survey by Adoptive Families magazine, most adoptions through private agencies happen within six months. The survey shows that 42% of private agency adoptions "matched" within six months; 22% matched between six and 12 months; 11% matched between 12 and 18 months; 9% between 18 and 24 months; 9% between two and three years.

Seven percent took three years or longer.

We were in that 7%—Lucky Number 7, baby!

Every reputable agency should provide its annual placement statistics to show realistic expectations about wait time and other factors. How many boys were placed? How many girls? We received a similar spreadsheet when we were originally comparing agencies.

The waiting was relentless. We understood the lead time, which by human baby-making standards took about 9½ months. Private adoptions took longer, with the national average being approximately 13.7 months from initial inquiry to placement. On top of that, legal finalization can take an additional 4-to-16 months after placement, according to the Rudd Adoption Research Program at the University of Massachusetts Amherst.

To survive this purgatory waiting period, I threw myself into my work as a diversion. That was the easy time of day because of the natural flow of distractions. The harder part was after hours—what to do in the unbillable parts of the day like early mornings and late nights. Aside from my teen years, when I used to work out to Jane Fonda in preparation for summer camp, I never had a burning desire to exercise—until that point.

Now, the morning alarm clock would chime and I would stagger out of bed to begin my new running routine. By the time I reached the end of the block, my anxiety would start to pulse, and my walk would shift, first to a gallop and then to an all-out run. My angst was so high, this would eventually become my method to control my madness. It was not uncommon for me to repeat this effort again in the evening.

These quiet moments allowed me time to reflect and wrap my head around our adoption progress, or lack of progress. Planning getaways and family vacations became more complicated, never knowing when we might be "called" by a prospective birth parent, or if a stork would miraculously drop a baby onto our doorstep—my hidden wish. There was always the possibility of an unplanned delivery; but as long as we were a hop-in-the-car moment away, or a 2-to-3-hour plane ride from home, I always felt comfortable.

To stave off disappointment but keep the delivery expectation alive, we cleared out our middle bedroom to make room for a nursery. It remained barren for two years. When things began looking brighter, we ordered a crib, but it stayed in the corner in its box until we were sure about our baby. I would spend a lot of time on Pinterest and other sites collecting baby room ideas. This was a fun outlet—I knew my baby would come. It was just a matter of time. Decorating ideas would mush in my head until we finally connected to our birth parents. Then it would become real and the unboxing ceremonies could begin.

PLACE
2ND

08

Passed Over

A potential match can come any time. No warning, no time to collect your thoughts. At least that's what it felt like when our agency informed us that we were one of two couples a birth parent was considering.

It was electrifying and terrifying all in one brief moment.

Our agency was very forthcoming and let us know that we were number two on the birth mother's list. She wanted her child placed in the home of a gay couple. She had plans to travel the world and enter the Peace Corps and had no intention of keeping the child.

The birth father, on the other hand, was in love and wanted to parent with the mother. From what I understood, he was somewhat manipulative; she wanted out and away from him and this was her way to do it. He promised to let her go if he could be part of the selection process. From our brief qualifying stats and a quickly thrown together profile book, he liked us best and was in our corner.

We scheduled a call between his shifts at work. I had a list of questions in front of me in case I had a lapse in memory, which would not have been atypical, given the high stakes.

Tell me about yourself.
Tell me about your family.
Tell me about your current job.
What are your hobbies?
What do you enjoy doing in your spare time?
What were your favorite subjects in school?

The list was there to keep the conversation flowing in case there were awkward moments. Fortunately, we really didn't need it because this birth father was very forthcoming and shared quite a bit without us asking. He asked us questions along the way, including my music preferences. I told him I liked R&B but I couldn't recall any group names. Ugh! Flo Rida popped into my head because I had recently come from a run and was listening to Pandora. When I asked him the same question, he responded that he preferred classical music. I definitely was not prepared for that one.

The conversation lasted about 30 minutes but in the end the call really didn't matter. The birth mother had already connected to the other couple and we couldn't compete. She did not even want to have a conversation with us. We quickly learned that the birth mother always wins.

"Tell her we're the second-best thing to a gay couple without being gay!" I shouted to the agency. That didn't seem to work. I was sad but not too sad because I empathized with the struggles of the other couple. I wanted them to have a family. In the meantime, I had to keep faith that our baby was out there waiting for us.

Chris and I had our fair share of roller coaster moments. We tried our best to remain open and positive throughout the process but there were some bad days. After a few close matches that ultimately fell through, we learned that dark days were part of the journey. We came to understand the importance of staying fluid with the back-and-forth dialogue and sharing honestly, even if it made us blush at times.

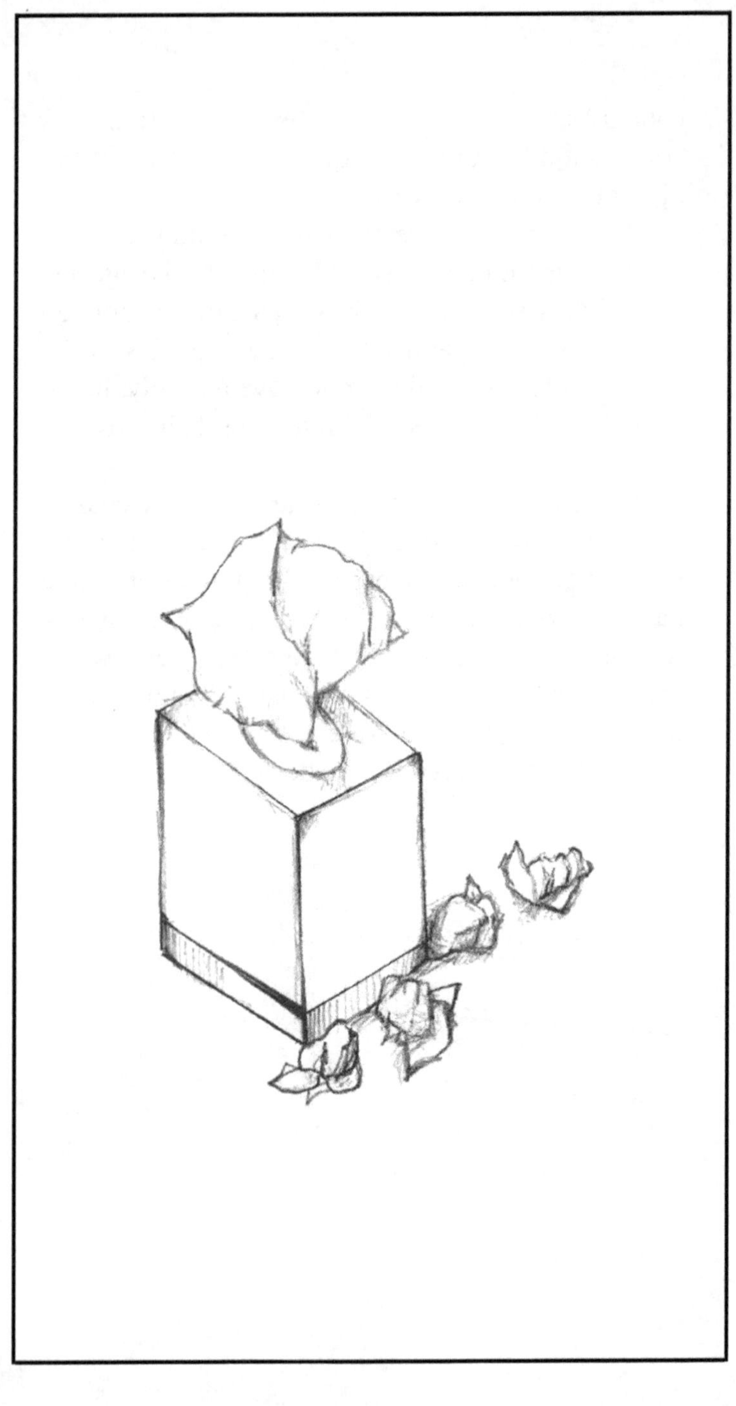

09

A Hard Pass

On my birthday, May 21, 2014, we got the thrilling call we had been waiting for.

Or at least the call we *thought* we had been waiting for.

We were in New York City for my best friend's daughter's bat mitzvah weekend when my phone rang. It was the director of our agency! The birth mother of a healthy baby girl had selected *us* on *my* birthday. I was awestruck.

But there was a problem: The beautiful baby girl had been conceived as the result of a rape. When Chris and I spent hours with the agency's questionnaire, developing our parameters, we decided we would not consider adopting a child whose father had raped his or her mother. We did not want to have to tell our child that he or she was conceived out of anger or abuse. Neither one of us had this type of experience and could not fathom the future conversation. We were also aware that with rape, there would be other hidden issues with genetics, and we did not want to take that chance. We were very clear about that, and we made it clear to our agency.

But the agency considered this an "exceptional" case. Would we consider it?

The agency director, moving at a super-fast rate, acknowledged it was a last-minute decision. This young woman had just given birth and they were alone at the hospital. In her defense, the director thought we might be open to the case after hearing this birth mother's story.

The crime was not committed by a stalker lingering in the corner of an old shopping mall taking advantage of an unsuspecting woman walking past. Rather, two college students who knew each other were at a fraternity party. The birth mother believed a drug had been slipped into her drink. This woman was about to graduate from a major university in Austin. She was an intelligent, attractive ballet dancer with a sweet disposition. She knew the perpetrator but decided not to press charges. She wanted to move past the "incident" as fast as possible.

This had to be a sign, right? After all, it was my birthday.

We had a few hours to think it through before a scheduled call with Amy, the birth mother. I remember sitting in the car as we made our way to our hotel. Chris and I sat in silence as we crossed the George

Washington bridge from New Jersey to Manhattan. Tears streamed down my face—a combination of extreme hope and pure anxiety. We just arrived in New York City and I was ready to head straight back to the airport. I thought to myself, "I don't want my baby going into foster care! I've got to get there *now*!"

We made our way to our hotel in Times Square, where we contemplated the issues. In the comfort of this generic hotel room, where thousands of people had slept, I felt confident we had found our baby. Chris wasn't so sure. I sat on the sofa, staring at the clock that seemed to tick way too loud. *Tick. Tick. Tick.* There was a lot of back-and-forth conversation followed by a lot of silence. Painful silence. Day turned to dusk. I wanted this child and was ready to commit. I could almost feel her cuddled in my arms. I could smell her sweet baby skin. She was my birthday present, a true Godsend and answer to my prayers. I kept looking at the clock. We had to make a decision. Are we a "YES!" or a "no?"

Until that point, Chris and I had not discussed the variations of rape. It was just a solid no. I was ready and willing to let that go. I related to this woman, at a frat party—probably a lot like parties that I had been to during my days on campus 20 years earlier. I realized my original definition of rape had been the "stranger rape" definition, whereas Chris was uncomfortable with a child who was born as a result of a date rape.

I tried everything under the sun to convince Chris this was our baby:

"They're college educated kids—they have smarts and pedigree!"

"How can this not be a sign? It's my birthday!"

"The wait is over!"

Chris just couldn't do it. It was the hardest thing in my life I had to say no to. I had to remind myself that we were a team and in it together, but that was probably one of the saddest, most poignant times in my life.

Tears poured down my cheeks as I called the director of our agency and told her we had to pass. She was very matter-of-fact. She said she'd let the birth mother know and would move on to the next couple on her list. The wheels were now in motion and we were out. I was devastated.

That night, we went to my friend's townhouse and I received an unexpected call from the birth mother. The agency left a voice message on her cell phone that we had opted out but she had not received it. I heard Amy's voice and froze with the phone in my hand.

"Oh my god—what am I doing?" I said to myself.

This unassuming young woman did not get past hello.

I hung up the phone and cried hard for hours upon hours. I am not sure I slept that night at all.

All I could think was, "Did I just give away my baby?"

It was such a devastating moment. How did I hear the voice of a woman who wanted us to parent her newborn, and automatically hang up? Am I a terrible person?

These thoughts tormented me for the next two very dark days. Fortunately, we were in my favorite city and had many distractions. Even so, I barely slept for two nights. Saturday afternoon I took a much-needed nap and awakened with a sense of comfort and renewed zest for life.

For reasons that make adoption complex, personal, and challenging, I eventually came to the realization that this baby was not our match. From the initial "this is the greatest gift ever" euphoria to the "this is the cruelest joke the universe could play" devastation, I came to understand it was neither. I realized at that moment life was simply made up of intertwining paths.

Ten months later to that very day, our son was born. Source heard my prayers and answered them. Looking back, that was my first "Godwink." Call it faith or pixie dust sprinkled from above, that was the day I felt that I was being guided from a heavenly source. I was not alone on my uphill journey. Yes, we were challenged many times over, but we never lost faith. I kept thinking to myself, "my baby is waiting for just the right moment to be born." That could not have been more profound. I didn't know it at the time, but that's when my magic began.

VITAMINS
PRENATAL

10

The Start of Something Wonderful

It was Monday afternoon and as I was heading back to my hotel room for a break between sessions. I was in San Antonio for an executive retreat and it was siesta time. I had 30 minutes -- enough time for a quick snooze. I pulled out my phone to set the alarm when a call came in from a number in area code 512. It was our agency.

"Hi, Melanie, we've got some good news. You've been selected by a couple and you're their first choice!"

The moment was a little surreal. I quickly grabbed a pen and pad of paper on the desk to jot down notes. Couple's name (different from the pre-screen), due date, sex, genetic history.

"Wait! I need to conference-in Chris!"

Fortunately, he picked up on the first few rings and I blurted, “We’ve got a match!”

We started from the beginning once we were all patched in together. It all sounded too good. She was 22, he was 26. Both were college-educated, athletic, outgoing. He spoke multiple languages; she was in the arts.

“There’s a red flag somewhere,” I thought to myself as more good intel followed: family-oriented, wanted the best for the baby, prenatal vitamins started early in pregnancy. The list continued and I was in a bit of shock and awe.

“Why do they want to place the baby for adoption?” I asked, concerned. This was *my* red flag. We were told they felt too young and not ready. They wanted only the best for their child, and they couldn’t provide that at the moment.

Typically, matches were made after the seventh month of pregnancy. In our case, the birth parents were interested in planning ahead, so our match came earlier. That was not standard, but then again, each case varied.

“How many profiles did they look at before selecting us?” Chris asked.

“Nine.”

Now we were both a little peeved and thought, *We’ve been in line for over two years and you gave them nine options? Seriously!*

I hope we were given the same exposure when we were lower on the list ... like No. 11 or No. 12. I know it sounds pathetic, but it was the truth. There were about 15 couples ahead of us when we first joined our agency. We were told we would be placed at the back of the line and wait our turn unless there was an especially good "fit" or the birth parents wanted to see more profile options. In hindsight, if birth parents wanted to see 10 or 15 profiles, they would be shown 10 or 15 profiles.

After years of waiting, Chris and I were both a little disillusioned with our agency and the process as a whole, but we were too deep in the game to jump ship. We were, after all, now on top of this annoying "list." Yes, the list became super annoying. We didn't give it too much thought at the beginning. We were just happy to be on it. I remember the director saying how they needed more prospective parents in their repertoire. I thought that was a great sign—there must be lots of babies needing families, right? Wrong. What I came to learn was that if birth parents wanted to see more profiles, they'd see more profiles. Ugh! Super freaking annoying. We had zero power in this part of the process. Zero. Zip. Nada.

"Why us?" I asked, surprised. "They liked that you appeared athletic," she responded.

What?!

My heart probably skipped a beat as I started to laugh. "They must have us confused. What gave them that idea?"

I became a little worried that there was a mix-up—that the birth parents actually wanted some young, spry couple and got us by mistake. Ten years earlier we were probably at the height of our athletic prowess, way before my knees and his back gave out. We were both in our 30s and killing the gym scene. I was in my supersonic kickboxing phase at the same time Chris was a third-degree black belt. But then marriage and work and dogs and life got in the way of our physical fitness bubble. It was bound to pop.

Because we fall on the *under tall* side of the spectrum—I'm 5-foot-0 and Chris is a whopping 5-foot-4—a few extra pounds here or there has a way of looking twice as bad on us. We've always been aware of that, and we understood that exercise was a big part of keeping us in our proper zones. I knew we put lots of outdoor activities in our profile, but I didn't think we ever proclaimed ourselves to be athletes in any form. Maybe she meant to say "active?" Yes, that we were. Whatever, I just rolled with it.

"So what's the next step?" we asked.

The answer was a little scary: a call with them had been scheduled for us at 11 a.m. Sunday. We had a week to wait before we talked to them. I was a mixture of emotions—happy and nervous. This wasn't our first rodeo. We had two other potential matches by this point—the New York City birth mother debacle and the estranged birth father *megillah*. It was time to buckle up and get through the rest of the week. It was just Monday, and I knew it was going to be a hell of a ride.

11

She Likes My Smile

Sunday morning my eyes pop open. I look at the alarm clock and it's only 6:30 a.m. Too early for the *CBS Morning Show*. I love the trumpets at the beginning that herald the start to a new day and another week. I am enjoying the momentary silence before Bruce Lee, my sweet little Schnauzer, pounces on my stomach to greet me with a morning hello and tell me he's hungry.

"It's too early, Poo," I beg, but he doesn't seem to listen. My sweet Llhasa Apso, Phoebe, joins her brother on the bed. She walks on my face with her little fluffy paws. "OK! OK! I'm up!" I tell my furry little babies. "But you only get a snack."

Now I'm really up. I reach for the book a friend gave me to read a few months back, *The One Thing*. How appropriate. If I could just read One More Page without my mind drifting from topic to topic, I'd feel better. "Focus, Melanie," I tell myself, but, again, I only get through a couple of pages. I usually love this type of inspirational book; I have stacks and stacks of them, but I've been reading this one for a while without much luck getting through the first quarter of it.

Finally it's 8:30. Oh good—time for my lovely CBS Morning Show. "Aw, man. I missed the trumpets!" I say to myself with a pang of sadness.

When 9:30 arrives, my mood shifts away from watching the Sunday political shows. I've had a small crush on George Stephanopoulos since his days in the Clinton White House. "Sorry George," I say as I click off the TV.

I turn to Chris and ask, "Want to go for a walk?" He has no intention of moving.

The day looks amazing. It's perfect. Kind of reminds me of the movie *Mary Poppins*. The birds are singing, the sky is electric blue, the air is crisp. My favorite type of fall day. The sun casts a beautiful light glow on everything. But I'm no Mary Poppins. My heart is racing, and I feel like I will pop out of my skin.

I turn on Runkeeper, place my earbuds in just the right spot and start my walk. Usually, when I feel like this, I'll start to jog as I repeat my personal motto, *"My body is like a Cadillac—built for comfort, not speed."* But today I've got too much on my mind. I call my mom.

I start with "Hi. How ya doing?" small talk as I try to keep cool and not show too much emotion. For the past couple of years, I have not shared too many details of possible matches beforehand. This is not because I'm trying to hide anything but to protect myself and save my family from hurt and pain when things don't go as planned.

I'm not sure why it was different this time. She knew why I was calling but we didn't go into much detail. Rather, I asked about the Alaskan cruise we had planned to celebrate my father's 75th birthday. What if, by sheer miracle, we have our baby? "When are we going?" I ask as I try to calculate how old our bundle would be, hopeful that we'd be past the three-month point. "June, I think; you should really call and ask your father." "I think you're right. Yes, June—it's somewhere on my calendar," I reply, not intending to make that call.

We chat a little longer, talk about the Thanksgiving weekly schedule: Wednesday night/ Susan's for Mexican dinner. Thursday day—Rachael's for round No. 1; dinner—Pam's for round No. 2. Friday night—Shabbat dinner with everyone at my parents' condo. My *thass* (that's my thigh-and-ass) is growing larger as we speak about the gluttonous extravaganza.

Our call ends and I'm only 1.5 miles into my walk with a ways to go. I still feel the need to talk and I know my dad is driving around with his dogs and smoking a cigar. Typically, he'd be on the golf course but the rainstorms this past week have made it too damp to play.

I take a deep breath and call my father. "Hi, Dad, whatcha doing?"

"Nothing. Just driving around, smoking a cigar with the dogs. They are really happy."

"Oh, that's good" I respond, hoping to tread lightly on our conversation but knowing deep down that's not going to happen.

"So, are you ready for your call?" he asks open-endedly. That's one of the many traits I inherited from his gene pool—the art of cutting straight to the chase.

My heart starts beating faster as the questions flow. Now I'm really nervous. I've been so preoccupied this past week that I've kept my mind free from worry until now.

"Tell me again about them?" he asks.

"I think she's in the arts. Maybe dance?" "Oh, that's great! You can tell her that your grandfather was a past chairman of the Austin ballet."

Hmmm. I didn't know that. Maybe I can throw that into the conversation somewhere? Will need to store that in the back of my brain.

"What about him?"

"He says he's good at languages and economics. Really into sports, too."

"That all sounds really good! You can tell him you grew up going to every Rice game."

Hmmm. Not sure that will really help me, but I think we may be on to something.

I ask about different sporting events. I think this could actually help me connect to the birth father, but then I start getting confused with all the stats my dad is throwing out, and my brain shuts down.

"Okay, gotta go," I say.

"Good luck. Call us later and let us know how it goes."

"Will do—bye." I hang up.

I feel overwhelmed and now I'm in full-out tears. Shit! I knew this would happen. I'm a mess. I look at my watch. It's 10:30. I have another mile to walk home. Okay. Who can I call? Need to talk. Need to talk. Need to talk!

My friend Stephanie usually is out at this time while her kids are in Sunday school. I frantically begin calling her and, fortunately, she picks up after a few rings.

"Hey, do you have a sec?" I ask. She knows something is not right.

"I'm having a moment. I'm a mess! My call is in 30 minutes and I have to get my shit together."

She's been through this before with me and knows my status. She coaches me through the next few minutes. "Breathe ...breathe ... breathe," she says in a calming voice. A few minutes pass and I start to feel better and more confident.

My watch says 10:45. I've pulled myself together and I head home. Before I reach the house, I quickly scan my Pandora playlist. Who do I listen to? What bands do I like? A guy had asked about music in our first birth parent call a couple years earlier. Back then I blurted out Florida. I want to be prepared this time—just in case.

Let's see, do we want pop rock? Maroon 5?

Bruno Mars?

How about Hip-Hop? Macklemore & Ryan Lewis?

Who's Pitbull? Flo Rida? Softer? Sara Bareilles? Adele? Jason Mraz? Classic 70s: Duh. Elton John.

Motown: Supremes, Jackson 5, Gladys Knight.

Old school favorite: Sinatra.

Time's up. I walk through the front door and yell, "Chris, you ready?"

It's 10:59. Chris and I look at each other and then start dialing.

"Hello?" Chris and I blurt in tandem. My heart is racing. There's a momentary silence on the other end and then two voices respond. "Hello!"

Oh my god, they're actually there! And we have them together? Unfrappin' believable.

"How are you?" I ask as three other voices say something similar but different at the same time. We all seem to be speaking nervously over each other and nobody can decipher who is asking what.

Chris looks at me and mouths for me to let them speak. I back off.

"How's the weather where you are? I hope it's as beautiful there as it is here," Chris says.

Why does every conversation always start with the weather? It's so base and simple. The least common denominator we can relate to, I guess. However, it really is beautiful and crystal blue here in Houston. I realize that I really do hope their day is equally as pretty in Austin.

"Yes, it's great where we are, too," Kevin replies, taking the lead in the conversation.

"So, we want to be very honest with you. There is another couple we're also talking to after this. We both like you but want to keep our options open. The other couple has kids, and Elizabeth really wants to find a home where there are no other children. On the other hand, I'm from a big family and want that type of home for the baby. I like that you seem to have a very large extended family."

"I'll take that," I say to myself.

Okay. He seems very thoughtful. Very well spoken, too.

I'm picturing a large, athletic and handsome man with wavy brown hair on the other end. I would say tall, *dark* and handsome but I know there is some Irish in his blood, so I opt for pale skin. There is also a confidence in his voice. It's strong and assured. I like that. On the other hand, there seems to be a discernible gentleness in his voice—a softer side. From the brief moment he's been talking I feel like his character is coming together for me.

Elizabeth has been very quiet up until this point. I'm getting a little nervous.

"Why don't we start by going through your profile book. Do you have that with you?" Kevin asks.

"Um, no, but it's in the other room. Chris is grabbing it now," I tell them.

Wow. I wasn't expecting that but okay, I'm going with it. I thought we'd talk spontaneously, like we did on our first birth parent call a couple of years earlier.

How different could it be? Very different, I quickly learn. Interestingly enough, both calls were guided by very strong male personalities, but the tone varied on this one from the onset. Kevin was very intentional and direct. And he wanted to go through our profile book, page by page.

We're about ready to open the book when Kevin comments on the cover. "Elizabeth really liked your picture. She didn't even open the book and told me you were her first choice. I said it would be good to *actually open and read it* before making that decision, but she seemed pretty adamant."

The photo he was referring to was a quick selfie Chris and I took standing on the cobblestone streets of Florence, Italy. I was wearing a woven hat that I had just bought at the nearby flea market. Chris was in his standard baseball cap.

I hear tears on the other end. A soft feminine voice speaks up, "I fell in love with your smile."

Oh, thank God—she's there.

My fear had been that I had lost her in our very brief opening. Those words were the validation I needed, and a burst of new energy emerged.

12

Miss Sunshine

My smile. Elizabeth was referring to the automatic facial expression that emerges in pretty much every picture I've ever been in. I've always had the same pose. As a little girl in ballet class, my teacher, Miss Peggy, nicknamed me "Miss Sunshine" because of it. I would be standing in line in my light pink tights and black leotard, unsure of my next move.

This would pop into my 7-year-old brain:

Am I supposed to go right then point? Or point then hop right?

Confused, I'd sneak a glance at the kid next to me to see what she was doing, and I'd catch Miss Peggy staring at me—she must have figured out that I had absolutely no idea what I was doing.

So I just smiled in embarrassment—all the time. Like putting a period at the end of a sentence.

Being the smallest dancer on stage, I was always the one at recitals who was placed at the end of the line and gave the last wave and kiss to the audience before running off stage. It must have been there—in between swimming and dance lessons, where the seeds to my self-awareness were firmly planted. Compared to my peer posse, I was small in stature, and thick-boned. Fluffy legs, early-bird boob buds, and a short bob haircut only added to an already awkward adolescence.

As years passed and other awkward experiences piled up, I kept smiling. The automatic facial expression that seemed to shine light to the outside world became my way of coping with the world around me. My natural smiling reflex eventually became my way of dealing with the world around me. I learned that in difficult times I could hide my true, gut-wrenching feelings behind my easy smile.

By nature, I have a sunny personality. My mother, whom my dad nicknamed *Mary Fucking Poppins* who-knows when, is the same. She can light up a room with her glowing smile and warm disposition. People from all walks of life are naturally drawn to her.

My father, on the other hand, is a matter-of-fact, take-it-or-leave-it kind of guy. His sailor's mouth suits him in a lawyerly kind of way. Getting him to smile for a photo is like pulling teeth. I often have to remind him to lighten up for family. Interestingly enough, he holds court in a similar kind of way as my mom, but instead of smiles and an endearing hug, my distinguished father charms people—and gets them to laugh—with crude jokes.

Then there's me—a pretty good juiced-up combination of them both. My personality typically shines through my smile, which eventually leads to an opening hug when first meeting—whether I've known you for 20 years or two minutes. That's my mom. I also have the gift of gab with the occasional bit of salty language sprinkled in for color, pending my audience—à la dad.

This DNA combination has served me well, especially when dealing with turbulent times in my youth. I could hide anger and resistance to a certain point, then—when I could no longer hold up appearances, the dam would break and tears would pour like Niagara Falls. That's me—an oxymoron, just like my Gemini astrological sign proclaims.

Many moons later, my smiling coping mechanism would help me, yet again. After the disappointment of not being able to have a biological child, I prepared to battle through the turbulent adoption frontier. I set my intention on my beautiful child, with a battle hymn in my head and a smile on my face.

Dear Birth Mother

13

Family Isn't Always Blood

Chris and I are leaning hard into our kitchen island, our eyes focusing like lasers on the cell phone between us. The voice changes back to Kevin. "You'll have to pardon Elizabeth. She is very emotional, and this is hard for her. To give you a little background, when we found out Elizabeth was pregnant we thought it would be easy to 'take care of it.'"

The implication was clear: their first option had been abortion.

"We went through the motions, but in the end, Elizabeth couldn't go through with it. You see, she was adopted as a baby and the thought of abortion was too painful for her. I understand and respect that decision."

Chris and I nod to the cell phone that's in speaker mode on the counter.

"I'm not sure how much you know of our situation. We're not together. Elizabeth is still in school and I am trying to focus on my career. I'm going to be moving out of the country soon and the most important thing for me is privacy. I have different plans for my future."

Chris responds, "Melanie and I completely understand."

Kevin continues, "I want to be very clear about this. I do not want this child showing up on my doorstep 15 or 20 years from now when I have a family of my own. I may change my mind down the road but, as of this moment in time, I'd like for you to respect my privacy."

I chime in, "Absolutely. We get it 100 percent."

He continues, "Elizabeth feels differently.

She'd like photos and updates."

At that point, Elizabeth quietly spoke. "If it's okay with you I'd like to get an update every so often. If you send pictures, I'll put them in a special box tucked away. I just want to know how the baby is doing and that he's happy. I promise I won't bother you. Maybe at some point, when the baby is old enough and the time is right, we can meet."

My heart went out to her.

Chris responds. "Of course, we'll send pictures and updates. Even videos if you'd like. We want to do what is right and healthy for our child."

I interrupt, "But we also want you in our life! You will be in our home and our hearts whether you know it or not—in the mornings when the baby wakes up and at night when he goes to sleep. You will be a part of us."

Chris jumps in again to clarify, "We can establish times to talk, Skype or meet you with the baby. You might want to celebrate birthdays or some holidays and we can arrange for that when the baby is older."

"Don't misunderstand," Kevin says. "We don't have any intention of parenting."

"And we don't want to co-parent." Chris continues. "The most important thing is that our baby and Elizabeth can connect when appropriate."

Kevin, wanting to keep the conversation moving, says that he thinks we're all on the same page and that we should start looking through the book.

We open to the first page and Chris starts narrating.

Elizabeth joins the conversation, "I love the quote you have there. It is so me and exactly how I feel."

She was referring to the quote I found one morning sifting through notable inspirational phrases on the web. Chris had originally placed a quote from Princess Diana about every child needing hugs (or something like that) but I felt it was not personal enough. We replaced it with a more meaningful thought:

"Family isn't always blood. It's the people in your life who want you in theirs; the ones who accept you for who you are; the ones who would do anything to see you smile and who love you no matter what."—Anonymous

That hit home for me, and I was glad it did for her, too.

We turn the page. On the left there's a large black-and-white photo of us taken when Chris and I were engaged. The photographer captured us in a gentle contemplative moment. My head is resting on Chris's shoulder and we both are looking down. For us, it's a quiet moment that was beautifully captured in time. To the right is our Dear Birth Mother letter.

I don't know why, but I never expected that we would have the opportunity to talk with both birth parents at the same time. I'm now feeling a little guilty that we did not address the letter to both of them.

Dear Birth Mother,

Welcome to our book! We are Melanie and Chris Promecene from Houston, Texas, and have been married for five years (seven at this point). We are reaching out to you in hopes that you might be able to answer our prayer to grow our family through adoption.

We understand the decision to place your child for adoption is one of the hardest yet most loving, unselfish things a person can do. With that in mind we are writing to you with an open heart and loving spirit.

Should you select us as adoptive parents, we want you to know that you will always be held in the highest regard and our child will know that he or she came from a very loving and caring individual. If you choose, we are open to having an ongoing relationship with you. We promise to encourage and support our child emotionally, spiritually, and intellectually, honoring his or her unique qualities and heritage. As parents, we will do everything in our power to provide a beautiful life for our child.

With love and admiration,
Melanie and Chris

Elizabeth begins talking again. "I loved your smile on the cover, then the quote. But when I read this letter, you had my heart."

I told her it came from somewhere deep within me and I'm glad she liked it.

Next page.

There's a full-page image of us with our whole family under our wedding chuppah. Elizabeth comments on how beautiful everything looks. We start telling them about our wedding, the planning, the place and how there was the largest, most amazing harvest moon I had ever seen as I walked down the aisle that evening with my father.

Kevin asks about the structure we are standing under, saying it's really unique. I'm about ready to talk about the Jewish custom of marrying under a chuppah when I look up and see Chris signaling the cut motion at his throat. He is obviously steering me away from this part of the dialogue since we'd been coached to stay away from anything religious—especially the Jewish stuff.

I quickly change gears and tell him that we designed a space that symbolizes the house where we will be merging our families. That, in itself, is the truth, right?

He seems happy with that response, so we continue to the following page.

Oh, Lordy, it's my page and all about me.

Fortunately, Chris talks on my behalf.

He tells them that I'm a fifth-generation Galvestonian, moved to New York City after college and studied design at Parsons. I'm super-close with my family, love my job, love my friends.

Kevin asks about what I do at work. To simplify, I explain that my recent projects range from designing the interiors of offices to hotels. I also have worked on hospitals, performing arts centers, and universities.

Since I know he's into sports I mention that our firm is currently designing the new Marriott Marquis convention center hotel that will have a landmark Texas pool on the roof and will be one of the new downtown Houston icons when Super Bowl 51 comes to town in 2017.

"You'll see it when the blimp flies over it," I say.

He thought that was pretty cool.

I hope he will think of us when he sees the hotel on TV. Our son will be nearly two at that point.

I'm caught off guard by what Chris says next. "Melanie is the warmest, most loving

and genuinely kind person I have ever met. I feel lucky every day to be married to her."

OMG. Did he really just say that? I want to cry.

"Aww. Thank you. I promise I didn't put him up to that! Chris's first words out of his mouth most days are 'queso and chips.'"

I hear giggles on the other end.

Now it's Chris's page. He's still in the lead. He talks about his work in graphic design, how he is super-close with his family, has a passion for cooking, and loves to fly. He's trying to filter through the material quickly. Chris starts to turn the page and focus on the next section when Kevin interrupts and politely asks us to turn the page back for a minute.

And then Kevin shares with us what caught his eye and led him to us: It was the image of a kid's paper airplane at the corner of the page near the last paragraph.

"Chris has a pilot's license and loves aviation. He can't wait to help his son or daughter discover their own talents and passions."

"I thought that was pretty cool. Tell me a little more about that."

"Gliders mostly. Some engines, small planes. I started flying in high school. Not sure why my mother let me do it. Seems a little out of sync with how we do things today. I guess she knew I had to follow my passion."

Kevin and Chris continue to talk about plane types and catching currents in the wind to stay afloat. They seem to be connecting. I am somewhat in shock at how smoothly the conversation is going. I'm also super-glad the guys are talking among themselves. My brain is in overload.

There's a moment when Kevin realizes we're off track (due to all the talk about airplanes). He steers back to us and we move through the next sections—travel, our life together, our families.

And then we hit the spread on our traditions.

Since Thanksgiving is later that week we talk about our family and friends gathering each year on Thursday morning for a game of Turkey Ball (which has fluctuated through the years from touch football to Ultimate Frisbee to this year's kickball). People of all generations—plus their family pets—meet at the local elementary school field. It's a really fun time and my heart is always happy.

As we glide through the images on the page, Chris begins talking about Christmas.

"We host Christmas Eve every year. We started that tradition eight years ago—the night we shared our engagement with the family. Also, since we were the last to marry, all other holidays had been claimed. So, by default, Christmas Eve became our night, and we love it."

There's a big, chaotic image of everyone in our living room opening stocking stuffers, drinking prosecco with a touch of Chambord and enjoying the moment. Chris and I were instructed to put these types of family photos in our book—something prospective birth parents could relate to. The bigger the Christmas tree, the better. Other religious ornamentation, like Hanukkah menorahs and such, was not considered a good thing.

With that said, I tried to find as many pictures with crosses in the background and us sightseeing European churches.

Kevin says, "It looks like a fun time. Do you celebrate any Hebraic traditions?"

A voice in my head screams.

O-M-G, did I hear that correctly?! Did he really ask about Hebraic tradition?? Wow! I have never heard it phrased like that before. I thought we were on such a roll with the whole Christmas thing. Shit! The cat's out of the bag.

Chris and I freeze in place. We stand there looking at each other and, for a split second, I taste panic. My mind races yet again as I try to carefully weave the right words into our backstory. I take a deep breath, look at my husband, and tread carefully with my words. I realize we have to address the dreaded topic of religion.

"Um, yes! We celebrate Hanukkah, too. I was raised Jewish, but we always enjoyed Christmas. That's when the big presents always came out."

Kevin laughs. Elizabeth is silent.

In a more serious tone I continue, "Chris and I are both very spiritual people."

That's the truth. I don't think it's necessary to dwell on the fact that Chris does not believe in organized religion or that our baby will be raised Jewish.

Chris jumps in at that point to ensure the train doesn't jump the track.

"I was raised Catholic. My entire family is very religious. My mom still goes to church every day at the age of 85. We will raise our baby to have an understanding of both of our religions. He will grow up with a backbone of tolerance and faith."

I'm biting my fingers when I hear Kevin say, "That's great."

I'm not sure what came next, but we move on to the next page. I feel a huge sense of relief that we got, in a sense, Kevin's blessing.

We've been talking nearly an hour and we're almost to the end of the book. Kevin is trying to wrap up the call and says, "I'm feeling really good about this. I don't feel the need to speak with the other couple at this point. Not sure why we scheduled the calls back to back—that was probably not the best idea. This has been very emotional for us. I don't want to speak for Elizabeth, but I think we've made our decision. Do you have any questions you'd like to ask us?"

I've been holding my breath for a bit and say, "Yes, I have a question, if you don't mind."

Chris looks at me and I continue looking at the phone.

"Are your families aware of the situation?"

Kevin replies, "No. We're keeping this from them. If they knew they would want to keep the baby, and that's not what we want."

Elizabeth is speaking now. Haven't heard much from her during this call and I'm nervous she's wavering.

"I grew up in a small town. My parents are older and wouldn't understand. They are very religious and would expect us to marry."

"How are you planning to keep this from them? Will you see them over the holidays?" I ask, aiming for a sensitive tone.

"Yes, I'm planning on spending both Thanksgiving and Christmas with them, but I'll be wearing baggy clothes. I'm not showing too much right now," she says in a matter-of-fact way. "After that, I won't see them for a while."

I'm not sure how to respond with anything more than "OK." Chris and I know that there are some big holes in her answer.

Kevin, in an effort to wrap up the conversation, says, "We don't want to draw this out any longer than necessary. We're going to make our decision this week. You should be hearing something before Thanksgiving. I think we're both feeling good about this, but we need some time to process."

Chris: "No problem. We understand. Thank you for taking time to speak with us."

Melanie: "Yes! Thank you so much. Have a lovely holiday."

And with that, the call ends.

Chris and I don't move. I think we're both in shock that we got this far. Now it's time to assess, debrief and totally tear apart the entire conversation we just had

"I think that went pretty well," Chris says. "I thought your timing was a little off with your questions at the end. We were on such a good roll and then the tone changed."

I get a little defensive. "I didn't want to be a Debbie-downer, but he asked if we had questions and I didn't want to miss that opportunity!"

"No, it was fine. But did we really learn anything new?" Chris asks, a little annoyed.

"I wanted to hear the plan from them," I respond quickly.

Taking a deep breath, Chris ends the conversation. "Well, it's over now. Let's get lunch."

We head to Cafe Express around the corner. I am not hungry but want to sit outside and digest the last overwhelming hour.

While Chris orders inside I find a table on the patio. I'm in deep thought when I turn my head and see Rabbi Pam from Congregation Emanu-El walking behind me. It's probably been about 10 years since I last saw her at a mutual friend's house. I think we're around the same age. I've always thought she was so kind. She's about to sit and enjoy lunch with her family but comes up to say hello.

"Hi! How are you?"

"Hi," I say back. I feel like a total zombie. I tell her we just finished a call with prospective birth parents, and I'm overwhelmed.

Not sure why I say this. Maybe it's because I know I'm a mess and I have nothing to hide.

"That's so exciting! I hope it works out for you."

"Thanks. Me too."

How ironic that Rabbi Pam is the first person I run into at the restaurant, especially as I'm dabbling in deep thoughts about our previous hour's conversation.

Should I be embarrassed by my hesitation to share my religious background with our prospective birth parents? I could blame it on our coaching. No—it's my truth, my life. It's what needed to be done to get me to this point. Maybe her being here is a Godwink that everything will be OK. I'd like to think so. Yes, I'm going to go with that.

I sit down and continue to ponder the rather odd conversation going on in my head.

I can't believe it. That was probably the most important phone conversation I have ever had. They seem young but at the same time very mature in their thought process. I like him. He sounds like he has a good head on his shoulders. Not sure if we'll ever hear from him again. I think he really wants out. She seems very sweet. I can tell she's hurting. I want to hug her. Is that weird? I don't even know her, and I want to hug her and ease her pain. But I want her baby. Is that terrible? This is so crazy. Our worlds are colliding with these two people we don't know, but who may become the most important people in our lives. This is so crazy....

And then Chris joins me.

We sit in the sunshine and enjoy our lunch together. Funny, we don't talk that much.

Lunch ends and we head back to the house. I reach for my phone to call my folks. They've got to be shitting bricks at this point.

There's a missed 512 number. "That's got to be our agency," I say to myself.

But it's not the agency. It's Elizabeth. And she wants us to call her—together.

I give the dogs another round of chew bones to keep them quiet, hit the redial button as fast as possible, and put the phone on speaker. We're back on the kitchen island, just as before.

"Hi, Elizabeth. It's Melanie and Chris! So sorry we missed your call. We were at lunch and I didn't realize my phone was in silent mode. Is everything all right?"

"Yes" she says. "There were some things I wanted to share with you that I couldn't say in front of him."

Chris and I listen intently. A stronger voice emerges from what we heard on the last call.

"First, I wanted to tell you myself that from the moment I saw your picture I knew you were the ones. I didn't want to make you wait any longer, especially during this Thanksgiving week."

How does somebody respond to that? The only words that came out were "Thank you!!! You made our day! Our Year!

"I have some images of the baby in utero I'll text you. They should be coming through now. I got these at my 20th week."

My phone chimes to tell me that a text has arrived, and I check to see what came through.

"Oh my gosh, I'm already in love!" There are two somewhat blurry images and an incredible 3D view of the baby. He has his little fingers in his mouth! Amazing!

"So what's the next step?" I ask.

"Maybe we can meet after Thanksgiving? I'm going to be out of town through Friday. Are you around Saturday?" It's as if we're old friends.

"Of course! We're here all week and can drive to Austin anytime!" I'm super-excited and can't control the enthusiasm in my voice. "We'll meet wherever and whenever you want! You pick the place and we'll be there!"

She continues, "I'd like to go somewhere quiet where we can talk. Let me think about it and I'll get back to you on the place. Maybe dinner Saturday night?"

Chris and I are both talking at the same time over each other. "Yes! Sounds great! We're so excited! Let us know when and where. Feel free to call or text anytime."

"Sounds good. Whose number is this?" she asks.

"It's my phone. You should probably have Chris's, too. It's 713..."

We're finishing an amazing conversation. How does one end a call like this? I hear myself thanking her.

"Elizabeth, from the bottom of our hearts, THANK YOU! THANK YOU!"

"You're welcome. Happy Thanksgiving and I'll get back to you soon."

"Goodbye! Happy Thanksgiving!" Chris and I both shout.

Our call ends. I look up to see Chris wiping away a tear. His eyes are a little red. I haven't looked at him at all during the call. I notice my eyes are watery, too. I walk over to hug my husband tightly and say, "This is happening. We're having a baby!"

It's a beautiful moment that I will always treasure.

PAWPAW'S
BAR-B-QUE
- EXIT NOW -

14

Our Birth Mother

My heart is singing. Truly, it is singing! I feel exhilaration at its highest peak. Aside from functioning on deprived sleep—no more than a few hours every night, my energy level is out of control. "How am I going to make it through this week? There's no how-to book on this one. I guess I'll eat my way through it? Yeah, that will work. It *is* Thanksgiving week."

The alarm buzzes at 6:30 a.m. Monday. Typically, I'd roll over and press the snooze button five or six times before slowly making my way out of bed. Today feels different. A bolt of lightning has me going at first light in preparation for the day. Since it's a short week I've made only a few plans. One is to meet with an old family friend I didn't realize lived down the block—or that there was a family connection—until a couple of weeks ago.

Noah and I met a couple of years earlier when he worked for the commercial real estate firm that represented my company during our relocation effort. Toward the end of the meeting, when cards were exchanged, I noticed his last name but for some reason didn't mention anything. Soon the moment fled.

Two years pass and it is now Election Day. Stopping quickly at the elementary school before work to cast my ballot I spot a familiar face in the relatively small queue. He's finishing as I'm coming through. We both stop and, recognizing a connection, begin friendly small talk.

"Hey! I know you," he says.

Relieved he is just as unfamiliar with me as I am with him, I exclaim, "Yes! We've met before. I'm not sure how we know each other. Do you have an office downtown?"

He shakes his head no then I ask, "where do you work?"

"Jackson Cooksey."

That's it! Y'all represented us in our move. You were in our office a couple of years ago. What's your name?"

"Noah Kruger. And yours?"

"I'm Melanie Herz Promecene. Are you any relation to the Austin Krugers?"

"Yes—that's my family. Why?" he asks. "My family is from Austin and…" before I could finish Noah asks all the whos, whats, and wheres to *finally* get to the part where our grandfathers were best friends. What a small world! I had heard about this wonderful family my entire life, and to just happen upon this connection was a really fun moment. Now that's "Jewish Geography."

"Okay, now that we're practically family" I say, "we've got to stay connected. Let's grab lunch sometime and connect more dots."

And so we lunched the week of Thanksgiving. Looking back, he must have thought I was a total nutball. In truth, I was a hot mess. Although I learned a lot about him during that soundbite session, he received a bigger earful from me and my pending date with our birth mother match. That's pretty heavy stuff for a get-to-know-you-session, don't you think?

I tried to keep as busy as possible the rest of the week. Fortunately, there were a lot of holiday festivities that helped me through it. We had the first of many family dinners on Wednesday, followed by Thanksgiving Thursday and then another family-and-friend gathering Friday night for Shabbat.

I was so happy that it was Friday—*finally*! That evening for dinner my mother had a wonderful Italian spread catered by Frankie Mandola, a local restaurateur and my father's old friend from Rice University. Funny, my mom does an amazing job of topping off a week of monstrous eating with, yes, *more eating*. This round, it's not just our nuclear family but extended family and friends—another fun night with loved ones we have not seen in a very long time.

I thought I was doing well keeping myself engaged and focused on the moment, but then my two childhood friends Julie and Andria whispered in my ear that I had my outfit on inside out. Good thing I was wearing black! The laughing brought about tears—which was exactly the release I needed at that moment. The mishmash led directly into our discussion about what I was going to wear to meet our birth mother the next day. For this clothes horse, my outfit would have a lasting impact well beyond our first date.

Honestly, I can't even remember now what I was wearing that day. I think we finally settled on jeans, boots and a leather jacket? For such a huge deal it's ironic that I can't recall the outfit as I write. Good thing there's a picture we took when we were together!

Saturday arrived. The drive to Austin was a bit nerve-racking. We had 2½ hours more to think about this first meeting. What will she look like? Will she like us? What if she doesn't like us? It was killing me.

Just as I'm pondering questions I might ask the birth mother; I look up to see my friend Andria passing us in her car as we zip along Interstate 10. She told us the night before she was heading to San Antonio, and it was a fluke that we were on the road at the same time. I took that as a good luck sign as she waved, honked, and sent love our way.

Halfway to Austin we stopped at Hruska's—a Texas landmark known for its bakery, beef jerky, and condiments. Our goal was to fill up with gas, hit the restroom and get some goods for the road but, damn—they were closed for construction. Ugh!

My plan of eating my way down the road just got interrupted. We drove onward to La Grange where I knew the Bon-Ton Bakery, another family-owned standby, would not let us down. I managed to buy pastries, cookies *and* candy. After all, I needed to keep my sugar stash up for sanity purposes. I was in full-force hand-to-mouth combat.

I have traveled the road to Austin hundreds of times. Years of visiting my Mimi and Pawpaw's house as a youngster and traveling back and forth from college made the road very familiar. I knew it so well that I could tell how long it would take to get to Austin by the trees in the road's median.

On our venture that day, after stopping to carbo-load, I was aimlessly looking out the window when I spotted one of those big message boards along the road. This one happened to say *Paw-Paw's* ahead. I blinked in astonishment, but we had already passed. I turned to Chris and asked, "Did that sign just say Paw-Paw's? I was just thinking about him and our trips to his house growing up."

I quickly turned to look back and see if it was there or if I was imagining it, but it was too late.

"That's really weird," I said out loud. "How many times have I been up and down this road and never once did that sign pop out until this very moment."

Regardless of what my eyes saw, I sensed that my grandfather was there moving me right along. I felt his hug and encouragement in that moment. I smiled to myself and promised to find that sign again on our way back. I had to take a picture.

I spent the remainder of the drive processing the charming Godwinks I encountered along the way. Finally we arrived at the restaurant Elizabeth selected for us. She had picked a popular casual eatery in Austin's Domain, a trendy shopping district. Elizabeth had arrived before us and alerted the hostess to our pending arrival. We were led to a table on the lively patio. Waiting for us was this petite, beautiful brunette with gorgeous, almond-shaped brown eyes. She was exquisite. I had to hug her immediately—it's what I do.

Chris and I were nervous, and I was an absolute mess. I let Elizabeth order for us. To my surprise, she ordered nachos—my favorite!

"I feel the magic," I thought. "I love her."

Hours flew by and the conversation flowed as if we were long-lost friends. One of the first things she mentioned is that her best friend is also named Melanie. Good sign, right? Through conversation I discovered she and I both love to Karaoke. When I admitted my song of choice was *Love Shack* by the B-52's, there were some laughs.

She told us about her relationship with the birth father, and I could feel her pain. She mentioned she had a new boyfriend, Henry. They had known each other as children and reconnected after he returned from Iraq a couple of months earlier. He knew she was pregnant and wanted to be with her regardless. I think he was in love with her for many years, and it was finally their time to connect. She shared that on their first date, he cooked lemon chicken. My eyes nearly popped out of my head.

"That's exactly what Chris made for me, too!" we chuckled together. *Wink.*

I was mesmerized looking at this beautiful woman and listening to her story unfold. As she spoke, I tried to understand her world and what she must be experiencing. She claimed to be a planner, which I thoroughly understood. That's why it was so important for her to finalize our match and meet in person. To me, these were all sure signs that we were on the right track.

About three hours into our get-to-know-each other date, I asked if she was calling the baby by a name. She looked down, then shyly looked back up and said, "Yes, I've been calling him Noah."

"I like that name," I said. "What made you choose it?"

"It's one of my favorites. When I think of a Noah, I see a nice, handsome, strong person." I had never met a Noah until recently.

Although I did not think of it until later, it was quite ironic that I had just lunched with Noah Kruger, grandson to my grandfather's best friend, earlier in the week. *Wink.*

I felt more and more comfortable as we spent time together. I wanted to hear everything about her but didn't want to pry. I have no idea how long we sat and talked—it must have been hours. At some point we decided that it was time to get the check.

"We might have overstayed our welcome here," I said. "Can we take a picture together? I want to remember this moment."

We headed outside and posed for a photo under a large, billowy tree. We placed that photo in our son's room the day we brought him home where it still stands.

After hugs and goodbyes, Chris and I headed back to our hotel in the Austin Hill Country. We were completely exhausted.

We sank into the lounge chairs in our hotel lobby and looked at each other. What a day. We were so tired that neither one of us could talk much.

We headed back to our room through the convoluted maze of hallways. "Who designed this hotel?" I snarked to Chris as we wound our way through the corridors.

"Oh yeah, I think my firm did. But that was way before me."

We weaved our way to our room, opened the door and found two queen beds. That was totally OK—a king bed would have been unnecessary anyway. We both needed space. I stripped off my clothes, hopped in the shower and then jumped into the clean, white fresh sheets.

"Oh, this feels so good," I said to Chris, who was reading his iPad in the other bed.

I was thoroughly exhausted at this point and my stomach was beginning to hurt. Maybe it's from the absolute shit I ate all day long. No—all *week* long.

So, I pass a little gas, right? WRONG.

Holy Shit! I jumped off the bed and onto the floor super freakin' fast. That was no fart. That was a supersonic shit!

"OH-MY-GOD I just shat the bed!"

Chris looked at me on the floor, not sure if I was crying or laughing.

Beside myself in absolute disgust and complete astonishment, I hopped up and stripped myself clean. I quickly jumped back in the shower and laughed my ass off. I guess I needed that emotional and physical release since somebody else was going through the birthing process for me.

"Man, they do not pay housekeeping enough.

Chris, we've got to leave an extra big tip."

Departing the next day, our heads hung low from embarrassment. We could not get out of there quickly enough.

"I don't think we can ever stay here again," I mumbled.

15

Coincidences—or Signs?

When we were on our way back home from Austin that Sunday, the sky was a little cloudy. It was drizzling but, in the distance, I could see the biggest, most amazing rainbow. No. Not just a rainbow, but a double rainbow! It probably stretched for miles. I had never seen anything like it. I tried fitting myself through our car's sunroof to take pictures of it.

"Nobody will believe me! It's too big to fit on camera. I've got to take a video."

That's what I did. I captured, on camera for all to witness, the most magnificent rainbow I had ever seen. I knew at that moment my baby sent that rainbow to me. Maybe my Pawpaw was holding his hand, too. *Wink.*

The closer we got to Houston, the worse the weather became. Some family members from Miami had been visiting their daughter in Denver and didn't know if they'd be able to get back home. They might have to stop in Houston for the night.

Of course, that is how the evening played out. When we got home, the call came in that all six Trents would be at our house that evening. So much fun! *Wink.*

In preparation for their arrival we put out all of the champagne glasses—and because our family is large and we celebrate often, we have a lot. Chris's mom and his sister's family, the Cooks, were going to join as well.

These impromptu dinners are a regular occurrence, especially since we all live nearby. Before the Trents moved to Florida, they lived around the corner to the right. The Cooks live across the bayou to the left. My brother's family lived in Memorial, a 10-minute drive. But it was a stormy Sunday night and the kids had schoolwork, so they stayed home.

Before the gang arrived, we set out lots of things to nibble on. Fortunately, we still had quite a bit left over from Thanksgiving. In preparation, I pulled out a silver bowl and placed a mango in it. The mango represented the size our baby was supposed to be, according to Elizabeth. I carefully wrapped this baby mango in a blue-and-white striped cotton napkin and placed him on the counter-top so he could be with the family when everyone arrived.

I stayed at home while Chris drove to the airport to pick up the family. While I awaited their arrival, I sat in my favorite chair by the fireplace and began researching the name Noah. The only thing I knew was that it was biblical. According to the Book of Genesis in the Old Testament, Noah, his family, and two of each of the earth's animals survived a world deluge in the ark he built.

Turns out there's a ton of stuff that comes up when you Google the name—especially the ark that Noah built for the great flood. As a designer, I looked closely at the architecture and dimensions that were in front of me.

Amazing how people have come up with pictures and diagrams of the biblical dimensions by the words in ancient text. Within every picture, the rainbow always shows above the ark, which brought back memories of our earlier drive home and the inspirational, heaven-sent rainbow that I knew was just for me.

After a while, I got out of the chair and moseyed toward the bathroom through a hallway filled with family photos. Some of our parents as children, aunts, uncles, cousins, the weddings of both our parents from the 1960s, and then ours hanging close by.

I stopped in my tracks. Our chuppah (which I always thought was designed a little odd but shrugged it off as a design from a quirky Galveston florist who had never built a chuppah until ours), looked exactly like the ark drawings I was just reading about. It had four posts with an open pyramid top.

I began to shake. Tears streamed from my eyes.

The chuppah is a Jewish symbol for a loving home that couples stand under during the wedding ceremony.

But *that* chuppah—*our chuppah*—was designed just like the Googled image of Noah's ark.

"I hear you, baby!" I said out loud as tears streamed down my face. "I know you're coming. You were there standing with us under that chuppah when your father and I married."

Now I'm beside myself. I have so many thoughts circling my head:

1. *Noah Kruger and I are newly acquainted neighbors and friends.*
2. *The coincidental moment seeing my life-long friend Andria along the highway to Austin.*
3. *Pawpaw was clearly telling me to keep going in the sign we passed on the road. I know he's watching how all of this is unfolding.*
4. *Our birth mother is calling our baby Noah and her best friend is named Melanie.*
5. *Chris and Henry both cooked lemon chicken the first time they made us dinner.*
6. *I just witnessed the most brilliant double rainbow my eyes had ever seen.*
7. *Our chuppah was designed in the same architectural geometry as Noah's in the Bible.*

Holy shit. I had to sit down again.

And I did. As I sat by the fireplace, I called my mom and babbled and talked and cried. She probably had no idea what I was saying. I'm not sure I made any sense.

"Are these signs from my baby? He's talking to me from above the rainbow! People will think I'm crazy. I would," I say in a quivering voice.

"Gotta go—the gang's here."

And then family burst into the house to celebrate and find out about meeting our birth mother. Everyone was wet, but the energy was abundant and electrifying. It really was a great way to end a very emotional weekend. With family—a support system –and (kind of) no judgment. They know I'm a little crazy.

"You've got to keep the name Noah," my niece Mia said. "It's perfect."

That was the moment we named our son.

Thank You

16

Under Investigation

Getting to know your birth mother really feels like dating on steroids. After our first lunch date, Elizabeth asked if I wanted to join her at the doctor for her checkup the next month.

"Would I? Of course! I'd love to—thank you!"

I was thrilled by the invitation and, honestly, hoping we might have time to get to know each other on a deeper level before the baby was born. I wanted to connect as much as she'd let me in her life. I didn't want to pry too much for fear of scaring her away, but I wanted to learn who she was as a person so I could, one day, report to my son if he asked questions.

That January, I first accompanied Elizabeth to the doctor. It was a quick day trip to Austin, and I was beside myself with excitement, not to mention nerves. I had never been to an obstetrics visit and was unsure what to expect. I also wanted to make sure our birth mother was going to a respectable clinic and under legitimate medical care. I felt a huge sense of relief as I pulled into the parking lot.

"Oh good," I thought. "I'd go to a place like this."

I took pictures of everything so I could remember the moment and share with Chris afterward. I had to be discreet, so in my best 007 covert way I managed to get shots of the clinic, from the exterior façade and entry to the interior waiting room, which was still cheery with holiday decorations.

Although Elizabeth had invited me, I was unsure of my place during the visit. She introduced me to her doctor as the adoptive mom, and that's just what he ended up calling me. "Mom, want to see the baby?"

Those words sounded weird but surprisingly natural the first time I heard them. I loved it. I also loved walking out the door with my own set of ultrasound pictures. I felt incredibly lucky that things were unfolding the way I had hoped. I would always be grateful that Elizabeth included me in that moment.

We followed the visit with lunch and more conversation. Since Chris was not there, it was more like girl talk. We ended up lunching again after the next doctor visit, too. It was a nice way to transition from an otherwise sterile experience. I think we both learn a lot about each other during those visits. Our comfort level with each other continued to grow during this gestational period. She mentioned how uncomfortable she was getting and, trying to alleviate some of that discomfort, I picked her up some soft pillows and specialty lotions.

I also treated us both to a relaxing spa day prior to the baby's arrival. I remember lounging in our robes in one of the anterooms before our afternoon of treatment began. We were having a great time, laughing and chatting. A woman sitting nearby pegged us as sisters. We shook our heads no, and she didn't quite believe it. "Funny," she said. "You look so much alike, too!" I smiled to myself.

The baby was due in March. In February, Elizabeth asked if we could have dinner together so Chris and I could meet her boyfriend, Henry. He was very special to her and had become a big part of her life since the baby's father was not involved. They did not want our first meeting to be at the hospital during birth. We planned a date around Valentine's Day.

I asked if they had any special requests and I believe that's how we decided on Chinese food. I made a reservation at a popular restaurant off Greystone Drive near Anderson Lane in Austin. My grandparents used to take me often when I was in college and I had fond memories of the place.

"Hope it's still good—I haven't been there in years," I told them. The last time I was there, I had dinner with my grandmother Carline, who lived in the neighborhood. Although my grandparents had both passed, I thought Carline and Pawpaw would have liked that we were at "their" restaurant. In hindsight, they were probably at the table next to us, eavesdropping and enjoying our conversation.

On our drive to Austin earlier that day and in preparation for the evening, Chris and I talked about what we would do if Elizabeth asked for alcohol during dinner. We concluded that we were not in a position to do anything, really. She was in her last few weeks and even my sister-in-law, who is a highly respected OB-GYN, said it would be fine if she had one glass of wine.

Chris and I were both excited about our dinner date. In a way, it felt more like a celebration. We decided to Uber to the restaurant because neither of us liked driving at night, especially through the rolling hills of a city other than our own. We arrived early and the hostess seated us at our table. Chris and I ordered a glass of wine and anxiously awaited Elizabeth and Henry's arrival.

They showed up about 45 minutes later. We exchanged big hugs, and Elizabeth told us how excited they were about the evening. We agreed the feeling was mutual.

Conversation flowed easily from the beginning as Henry thanked us for meeting them. "I'm so happy we could do this," I responded. "Elizabeth has told us so much about you, and it's great to finally meet you in person."

The waiter came to the table, noticed our wine glasses were empty and offered another round. Enjoying the moment fully, Chris and I both nodded yes. He then looked at Elizabeth and Henry and asked if they would also like a drink. At first, Henry said no but then, after we said it was fine with us, he ordered a beer. Elizabeth looked at me for approval and I said with my hands up, "Hey, it's your call. We're OK either way—you're almost done."

With that, she ordered her glass and sipped on it the remainder of the evening. We ordered appetizers upon appetizers, followed by numerous shared plates. I think the dinner lasted more than four hours, but it felt like two minutes. We really had a great time.

Toward the end of dinner Elizabeth mentioned how tipsy she felt. That glass of wine had been her first drink since she found out she was pregnant. Chris asked for the check and before the night was complete, we had our waiter take pictures of us so we could preserve the moment.

That night will be forever etched in my memory. But not solely because we had a wonderful time.

The next week, Elizabeth reported to our agency how much fun she and Henry had at dinner with us. Her caseworker, inquiring about the evening, began asking more and more questions—including whether anyone drank alcohol. Nonchalantly, Elizabeth said yes, and that she was really drunk. The caseworker asked how many drinks I had consumed. In the mindset of a college girl, Elizabeth guessed between 10 and 12.

The agency director, whom I had grown fond of over the past two years, called immediately. I remember being happy to see her number pop up on the Caller I.D., figuring she was going to deliver some great feedback about our bonding dinner. It was late afternoon and I was in my office.

And I was about to get a kick in the gut.

"I just heard some very disturbing news," the agency director said. "I have to begin an official investigation." She then told me what Elizabeth shared with her caseworker.

"Are you serious? No way could I consume that much in one sitting—I'd be on the floor!" I said, still thinking this could be dismissed with a big laugh.

"This is extremely serious, Melanie. As an agency, we need to make sure you and Chris will be fit parents. I am not sure we can place you knowing this occurred. Is it true? Why were you drinking with your birth mother?"

I've never been at a loss for words until that moment. I was mortified. Tears begin streaming down my face and I could barely breathe.

"Yes, we had drinks, but we were in no way drunk! That's just crazy! Why would she say something like that?"

I thought about the possibility of losing our baby. My head spun.

"I'll need to see the receipt from the evening, and we'll have to assess."

I explained that Chris and I had talked about the possibility of her having a glass of wine on our way to Austin that day. "We checked with doctors who said it would be fine!" I blurted out. "Birth mothers are in a different position, Melanie. They have their own set of circumstances that are unique from standard pregnancies."

"But you told us to connect and get to know each other in various ways—and this was natural for us. We were truly connecting!" I screamed through the tears that poured from my eyes.

I hung up the phone and immediately called Chris in high anxiety. He was in just as much shock as I was. I told him I'd reach out to the restaurant for a copy of the receipt. We needed an advocate now more than ever and I was happy we had signed up for Louise's "all-in" package.

This was gut-wrenching and humiliating. We might lose our baby over a college girl's senseless interpretation of what actually occurred during dinner. I cried for hours.

We shared our story with Louise who once again told us that in her many years in the business, she'd never heard anything like this. After a long conversation, she said she would stand by our side and do whatever it took to ensure our agency knew we were fit to be parents.

I felt a sense of comfort from her words as Chris and I thanked her for her support. We hung up and I got back to crying. My eyes were so swollen they were basically slits. My head ached, but I felt a bit of relief. Tomorrow I'd get that receipt from the restaurant as proof and we could put this issue to bed.

That's exactly what happened. However, I carried much anger and resentment toward the agency for a very long time. I can now say, after three years, that anger has finally released.

17

Delivery Day

At some point over the course of the past few months as I had grown closer to Elizabeth, she let me know she wanted me and Chris to be present at the hospital for Noah's birth. Not all birth mothers and adoptive parents have such a relationship and we saw it as a great honor. We couldn't wait for the day.

It was late Friday afternoon and my office was thinning out as coworkers headed home. I had just finished consolidating the basis of a design package for a hotel that was a potential client. I sat back and, with a sigh of contentment, logged off my computer. I was ready to go home. I'd been savoring these last few weeks as we wound into the final days before Noah's arrival. I'd had a standing 4 p.m. massage appointment to help me decompress through the weekend.

My world was about to radically shift. I figured I might as well enjoy my final hours of this chapter in pre-child life.

It was a glorifying afternoon of relaxation. A moment of bliss. Afterward, I sat in my car, turned on the motor, and pulled out my cell phone to check messages before going home. There was a call from Elizabeth:

"Hey! I just came back from the doctor and you may want to pack a bag. Baby may be on his way before the 23rd."

I called her in a bit of shock.

"Should we come right now? How long do you think it will be?" I asked, a little frenzied.

"I'm not sure. Just wanted you to know it's getting really close. Could happen anytime."

"Thanks for letting me know! I'm going to talk to Chris and get a game plan together. Please keep us posted! How are you feeling? Can we do anything for you? We're ready!" I said, excited.

I phoned Chris immediately. My formerly chill state was a memory. Fear and excitement exploded inside me.

My fingers can't dial the numbers fast enough. "Elizabeth just called and said she may be delivering early! I think we need to get to Austin *now*!"

My calm and reasonable husband had other ideas. "Hold on, wait a minute. What's happening? Take a breath. It could be anytime between now and Sunday—maybe even Monday or Tuesday. We'll talk about it when I get home. I'll see you soon."

My heart was pounding. I was ready to dart. I'd feel so much better if we could just get to Austin and hang out. I looked at my cell phone and started getting all the family numbers in place. There are a lot of us and I'm not sure if I have everyone's most updated info. I begin texting Chris and my sister-in-law Sharon to make sure my list is complete.

"Okay, good" I said to myself. I felt better knowing that I've got the major family peeps on call when the time comes. I got home and headed straight to the nursery. It felt so good. Over the past couple of years, I had stood in this exact spot for hours thinking about the perfect placement of everything, down to the yellow velvet glider and boldly-striped ottoman in the corner. It was a gift passed down from a friend that I happily accepted and reupholstered to imbue it with new life. I knew yellow velvet was not the most practical upholstery for a baby's room, but I didn't care. It felt soft and luxurious, and the color made me happy.

I thought about our baby. *He will like this room. I love everything about it.*

I opened the baby's closet and pulled out the items I'd been stowing for some time: a couple of tiny onesies and a few soft swaddling blankets. Although I had two outfits selected, I knew which one I wanted our baby to wear when he came home. I fell in love with a soft blue onesie with a lion's crest on the front. I spotted it a few months back and was reminded of my grandfather, Irving Leo Ravel (aka, Pawpaw).

Had we not decided on the name Noah, Leo was my backup. This outfit was in his honor.

Now it was time to pack for me. Unsure how long we'd be away, I carefully selected each garment—probably two weeks' worth of clothes. Overstuffing my suitcase is a habit I picked up as a child. Why limit yourself to a few items when you can have so much more to choose from? Chris argues that there's an art to carrying less, but I just roll my eyes and feel content with my 50 pounds of shirts, shoes, and accessories.

My clothes are packed, the baby seat is in place, and I'm ready to go. So where's Chris? He's taking his sweet time at the grocery store picking up some steaks to grill and wine to enjoy outside on the deck. He's in no rush, to say the least.

Chris arrives home and, as he prepares the meal, we discuss our plans for the weekend. Should we go tonight? Should we go tomorrow? Sunday? I'm a wreck, but Chris pulls me off the edge. We decide we'll head out in the morning. It's a beautiful Friday evening. We light candles and dine under the illuminated trees in our backyard. All is calm again and we appreciate one of our last dinners as a childless couple.

After our long, unwinding meal we decided to look into Airbnb. We found a really cool house off Congress Street that would let us have an extended visit. It's 11:30 p.m. and we're putting our card down to reserve the house starting tomorrow. My cell phone rings. It's Henry.

"Are your bags packed? Elizabeth is in labor and we just made it to the hospital."

"Really? How long do we have? Can we make it there in time for the birth? Tell Elizabeth to cross her legs and hold on! We're on our way!"

This is really happening. I'm about to
to hyperventilate.

Chris packs his bag then hops in the shower—which I think takes way too long.

"Seriously? You're taking a shower? We need to get on the road! If I don't make it to our son's birth, I'm going to be so mad at you!" I say with pounding conviction.

We finally leave Houston at 12:30 a.m.

Anxious to get moving—and being the better nighttime driver—I get behind the wheel and pull out of the garage. As we head toward Austin, what had been a quiet and peaceful evening morphs, and we find ourselves driving through one of the worst Texas thunderstorms I've witnessed. My already high anxiety level gets a little higher.

The storm is truly awful, and every few miles I see another car pulled over with lights flickering. The last thing I want to do is slow down, but the rain is so heavy, and there's so much debris on the road, I have no choice.

I think about gunning the engine, but I'm about to be a mom. A mom! The frightful drive feels epic.

After about an hour on the road, I ask Chris to let the family know what's happening. He says with a laugh, "Let's keep this our little secret until the morning. Won't that be funny?"

I'm not too impressed as I focus on the road at hand. "I guess there's no need to wake them at this hour," I say and drive on.

It's roughly 3 a.m. when we pull into the hospital.

Except it's the wrong hospital. Turns out there are several hospitals in Austin under the same umbrella healthcare company with similar names.

"There's no baby delivery at this hospital" somebody tells us.

Now I'm freaking out. "Where's the f-ing hospital? I can't be late!" I scream at Chris, who enters the hospital into our navigation system.

"It's only 10 minutes from here," he says as he gestures for me to back up and turn around. I thought I knew Austin but in the wee hours of the morning, things look really different.

We finally make it to the right hospital. We park and then run inside.

"Where's delivery?" we ask whoever is in our path.

Chris calls Henry on his cell. He texted us his number to keep us in the loop while we were driving. We wind our way to the room. Finally, I can breathe. We made it.

We knock on the door and quietly walk in. I kiss Elizabeth on the head and hug Henry. Her best friend, Melanie, is there, too. We find a place to sit down and attempt some chitchat in the now crowded room. Maybe a half-hour passes. We can see that Elizabeth is very tired and uncomfortable. It's been a long day for everyone. Chris and I step outside to give them privacy.

There's a built-in bench outside the room. It's long enough for Chris to lounge at one end and me at the other. The lights are low, and we begin melting into the cushion when Henry comes out, pulls up a chair and starts talking. I can tell there's a lot on his mind. We listen … for what seems like hours.

He shares stories about his family life, his military career, his ambitions. This tall, beautiful specimen of a man reflects on his time in the army, the friendships he developed overseas, and how he became disabled falling out of a Jeep in Iraq. Following his father's path by enlisting when he turned 18, Henry talks with reverence. His stories reveal true kinship, bravery, and a sense of honor to country. He is a much older soul than the years on his license indicate. At this point, his main ambition is to find a good, financially stable job and live a happy life with Elizabeth by his side. I couldn't help but compare his journey to my grandfather's and others who served during World War II. He seemed to be a throwback to the Greatest Generation.

Over the course of the conversation, Chris and I realize that we are old enough to be his parents. We both feel a connection to and love for him. Henry has taken great care of Elizabeth and we could not be more appreciative. For his love and attention, Chris wanted to give him something special. Knowing he and Henry shared a fondness for watches, Chris used this moment to pull out an old favorite—a black Torgen automatic chronograph pilot watch—and gave it to him as a remembrance.

Not long afterward, delivery began. Chris and I watched doctors and nurses with wagons of equipment parade in front of us and into Elizabeth's room. We were definite outsiders. "How many people does it take to deliver a baby?" we asked before humming a circus theme song. From our standpoint, we felt like monkeys eating popcorn as the show strolled by. We listened to the voices from outside the door but all I could hear were muffled sounds. I put my ear to the door so I could hear better. I was pressing so hard; my head could have pushed through the laminate. My eyes remained glued to my iPhone in an effort to record the exact moment I heard his cry: March 21, 2015;

6:14 a.m.—my baby is born!

It wasn't until later that we learned sweet Noah measured 21 inches and weighed 7 pounds, 7 ounces—statistics typically received the moment a baby enters the world. But we weren't in the room. A 7-foot high, 3-foot wide laminate door separated us.

18

Following Protocol

What a weird place to be. Our baby is finally born but we are outside, not even peeping in.

"Is he okay? Is everything all right? How is Elizabeth?"

So many questions and nobody to answer. Chris and I stand alone watching the doctors and nurses clear the way to quiet, yet again. Henry comes out a few minutes later holding our swaddled baby. With outstretched arms he passes Noah to me and I begin shaking. I am breathless and tears begin streaming down my face.

Within two seconds, a brusque nurse swoops down and removes my baby from my arms.

It's as if we offended her.

"Who are you anyway? This is not hospital protocol!" she blurts out.

Henry kindly says we are the adoptive parents.

She is not impressed.

"Follow me to the nursery," she barks. "You can't hold the baby, but you can look at him from the window."

Like little ducklings, Chris and I followed everyone around the corner to watch our baby being washed and weighed. Chris took a selfie of us in front of the nursery window—with baby in background. We texted this photo to our family. No words necessary. Lots of back-and-forth followed, and the excitement was in full force for the family.

My mother recently divulged that the time between Noah's birth and leaving the hospital was the most painful time in her life—even harder than losing her own parents. Had the situation been different, she—along with everyone else—would have been in the hospital with us. But that was not our story.

We had to wait the 48 hours mandated by Texas law before our birth mother could sign the papers which released Noah into our care. My mother's greatest fear was that we might not have our baby with us in the end. The selfie that we texted—the one Chris and I thought so endearing—had frightened her. My mother was well aware of the statistics. A large percentile of mothers committed to adoption change their minds after birth and end up parenting. We knew it, too.

I did not consider the anxiety and torment they must have experienced during our time in the hospital.

It pains me now to think of the angst they must have been going through. For all of us, I'm glad it ended up rosy.

YOU TELL'EM
NO YOU!
NOT ME

19

Modern Family

I feel nothing but love for Elizabeth. I think she feels the same about us. We have a very modern family; we are connected and will be forever. Our agency required us to send a monthly letter with photos during the first year, and then once a year until Noah turned three. But we've had more contact than that. I am very sensitive to Elizabeth's plight and I care about her wellbeing. After Noah's birth, she wanted to see frequent pictures. She was going through a mourning process, so I had to be careful not to overstep boundaries. Our baby was growing and developing into a beautiful little boy. She could take pride in that.

I cannot fathom the grief of giving away one's child. The closest I have come has been losing the idea of one. But that's just it. She gave us her baby.

During one of our visits before birth, she told me she never truly emotionally connected—that she had to distance herself and not get too close. I understand and respect that. However, our greatest fear was that once that beautiful baby was born, and she cradled him and changed his diapers and loved him and fed him, she wouldn't be able to let him go. After all, about one in three women who commit to giving her child to another family changes her mind and decides to parent after her child is born.

We were in a precarious position. Fortunately, Elizabeth invited us to stay at the hospital and sit with her, her boyfriend, her friends, and her family during this period. I truly enjoyed meeting everyone—it was a glimpse into her reality.

Chris and I did not anticipate meeting anyone in her family, especially not her parents. We spent some alone time with them in the hospital cafeteria, and we got to know one another better over coffee. It was surprisingly unawkward.

Elizabeth had planned on hiding her pregnancy from her family. But in her third trimester, her dad became ill with cancer. It became too difficult to hide her pregnancy while spending so much time with her parents and taking care of them. I can't even imagine the mental stress.

She eventually revealed her pregnancy and told her family that she had made plans for adoption. At the hospital, her mother told me how proud she was of her daughter for making that decision. As it turns out, our birth mother was adopted herself. Her mother was in my shoes 23 years earlier. I think Elizabeth's family was happy for us. I felt their support in the hugs we gave each other in the hospital.

The one thing that remained a secret to us was the fact that Noah was not her first child. Elizabeth did not want to tell us that she had a 3-year-old daughter, but we knew. We found out after visiting our family in Miami over the New Years holiday. Our college-age nieces and nephews were curious and did a little research on Facebook only to be surprised by this fact. Everyone in our family knew except me and Chris. They were not sure how to broach the topic.

Chris's brother Will got tagged to deliver the news. We were surprised but OK with it.

I looked at Chris and said, "This may help our situation, right? She knows what it's like to parent and understands the process and wants out."

I think if she and the birth father had been romantically involved, things would have ended differently. As selfish as it may seem I'm glad, for us, they weren't. Life would be very different right now.

With that said, you don't just get the birth mother, you get the family. This is not to say you must be close and celebrate holidays together. That is not it at all. We have our immediate family and that is enough. Instead, this is more like distant relatives whom you never really see but know about. Elizabeth and I are not connected on social media, but I am Facebook friends with both her mother and her sister. They know what's going on in our life when I share photos.

I must confess that at times, I look at our birth mother's Facebook page. I have a feeling she looks at mine, too. I am careful what I share online. I am very protective of my son and our family. I think this holds true for most people, not just those who adopt. However, as adoptive parents, we may feel slightly more attuned to boundaries.

ROSEANNE

20

More Signs

For two days, time seemed to almost stand still while we were at the hospital. We'd stay with Elizabeth as much as she'd have us. Chris and I appreciated every moment that was gifted to us. Sharing Noah and life stories made the time precious. Between feedings and swaddling, we'd hang out in her room and chitchat. The TV would play in the background without much notice until one moment occurred. A rerun of the '90s sitcom *Roseanne* was playing, and I could tell Elizabeth wanted to watch. She said it was her favorite show and that she bought the entire series to help her get through her pregnancy, binge-watching.

I told her I really liked it, too, and began telling her about a friend who was on the show after college.

"I think she played a cheerleader in one of the episodes, but I've never seen it."

Elizabeth perked up, "Really? I just finished watching that episode! What's her name? How do you know her? That's so cool!"

"Her name is Brandi and I was a camp counselor with her one summer in high school. We also ended up at college together—in the same sorority. She was a few years ahead of me. I was a freshman when she was a senior. She was always one of my favorites."

Then it hit me. Worlds started colliding.

I looked at Elizabeth and said, "I have a story to share with you."

I told Elizabeth that when Brandi turned 21 years old, she received a phone call. This was not an everyday, run-of-the-mill call, either. This call had been 21 years in the making. Brandi was adopted at birth, and on her 21st birthday her birth mother reached out to her. The woman on the other end of the call had told her she had been thinking about her baby girl every day since Brandi was born.

Since the adoption was closed, she had no way of getting in touch with her biological daughter. She had done a lot of homework to reach this call and it was not easy. She told Brandi that she had become a famous actress and asked if Brandi wanted to take a wild guess who she could be. She'd give her three tries.

At this point Brandi started to get excited. "Oh my God, are you…?"

"Are you…?"

"Are you Barbra Streisand?"

After three unsuccessful guesses, the woman on the other end of the line finally blurted out that she was Roseanne!

Elizabeth's eyes grow huge. She's listening intently. "That is so cool! I love *Roseanne*, and the cheerleader episode is my favorite!"

Now I'm a little wary about the accuracy of my story. I have the basic idea, but I wanted to get the details right.

"I really hope it was Brandi in that episode you were watching! I have no idea because I've never seen it—just heard about it all these years," I said to Elizabeth.

Elizabeth is now on her phone looking up the episode and trying to find my friend, the cheerleader.

"Shit," I tell myself, "I'd better be right."

Chris and I head back to our hospital room to give them some privacy. I go straight to Facebook and reach out to Brandi, to whom I haven't spoken in years.

03/22/15 1:52pm

Hi Brandi! It's been too long! Hope all is going well in your world! I know this is totally random, but you came up in conversation today...I'll try to keep long story short. My husband and I are at hospital with our birthmother who gave birth to a beautiful baby boy yesterday—sweet Noah. As we're hanging out in the room, *Roseanne* comes on tv. It happens to be our BM's favorite show.

She bought all seasons while on bed rest. So... you popped in my head and I shared the limited story I know about how you were on one of the episodes—cheerleader maybe? Anyway- they just finished watching that episode this week. Was that the one you were in?

Again, I know this is completely random but thought I'd reach out. I really hope you are well. You've always been one of my favorites...

Hugs and love,
Melanie

03/26/2015 7:23pm

Hi, my love,
I love that it happened that way. I have been thinking of you since hearing the news. Yes, I was the cheerleader, LOL. I am so excited for you!!!! What a wonderful journey you are beginning. I cannot wait to hear more about it! XO

That was all I needed. Affirmation that I wasn't losing my mind. She and Roseanne had become very close. She invited Brandi to Hollywood to work on the set after college and that's how she ended up on screen. One fateful day for Brandi and many years later, that episode is still deeply appreciated—on so many levels. Wink. Wink. Wink.

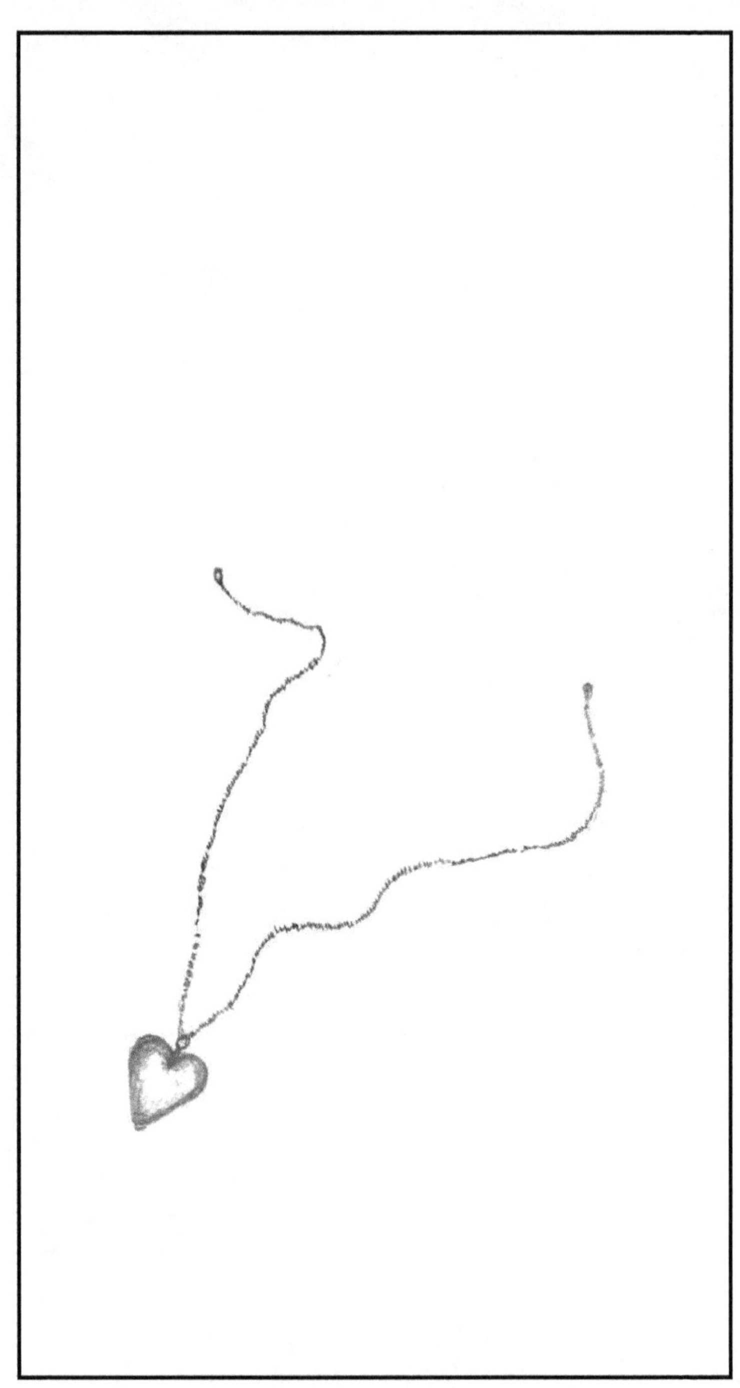

21

It's Time to Say Goodbye

I remember the day so clearly. The mandated 48 hours in the hospital had ended, papers had been signed, and Noah would soon be released to our care. Chris and I headed down the long, sterile corridor to Elizabeth's room. It would be one of the last times we'd be with her for a very long time.

We quietly walk in and see Elizabeth lovingly holding Noah. Henry is lying next to her and I can see Noah clutching his finger. Both Elizabeth and Henry are crying. Until this moment we've had a very sweet hospital stay, but now it is slowly drawing to close and the emotions are intensifying.

Chris and I take a seat on a built-in bench next to the bed. Henry's arm is relaxed against Elizabeth's belly and he is enjoying Noah's touch one last time.

I take note of Henry's bracelet. Elizabeth told me during one of our lunches before birth that she had wanted to give him something special to commemorate their first date. I asked her what she had in mind and she said she was having a bracelet engraved for him. The significance of this gift did not register until that very moment.

I spotted the engraved date on a silver plate, thoughtfully tied together with leather straps. It was lovely. I had to look closer.

What is the date? Am I seeing that correctly? My eyes stop and I contemplate the moment. I want to cry. Sitting in front of me was our birth mother and her beloved Henry, cradling with love and admiration our son Noah.

Nobody else knew it but me. In that moment my grandmother, Dorothy Ray Ravel, who had passed 20 years prior, was with us. She was telling me that she was there. The date on Henry's bracelet was her birthday, 9/9. She wanted me to know she was part of this experience. Though not physically present, she was watching from the other side and loving every moment. This was her gift to me. *Wink.*

I still cry when I think of that moment. I am crying now as I write. The gifts keep coming. The messages are real. They have been surfacing left and right and I am finally paying attention. I take a picture to remember this moment.

Before too much time passed, I pulled out a gift bag. Chris and I wanted to leave Elizabeth with something special, so we picked out a small necklace with a dangling heart from Tiffany & Co.

"I saw this and thought it would be appropriate. My maiden name, Herz, is German for heart. Elizabeth, you will be in our hearts forever."

At this point, we are all heartbroken. I can see the pain on their faces.

Elizabeth tells me it's time to take Noah and leave. Chris and I are unsure how to react. Henry hands me my child.

"It's time to go," he says.

I look back one more time and, before the door closes, I tell them, "Remember to dream big—like Roseanne big."

We closed the door behind us and walked out.

HOUSTON 150

22

Home at Last

Chris and I looked at each other in bewilderment.

"What do we do now?"

We're in shock as we walk around the corner and stand in the hallway with our baby.

We make our way to the nursery and open the door. A tall, heavyset nurse jumps up and starts screaming at us to get out. We are terribly confused. She briskly walks out to inquire what we're doing with the baby. We're obviously fish out of water. I don't know who is more startled—the nurse or us.

Standing outside the nursery we tell her that we've just been handed our son and want to leave.

"What's the protocol?" Chris asks.

My entire focus is on Noah at this point and I let Chris take over. I just want to get home now.

The nurse leads us back to the room where the hospital graciously let us camp for the past two days. This gigantic and scary nurse begins to calm down and helps us through discharge. She brings the official "It's A Boy" blue ribbon to our room and we finally warm up to each other.

I change Noah into the soft blue going-home outfit that I had picked out a few months earlier, carefully double swaddle him and prepare to leave.

Finally, we're heading out of the hospital. I stand with the nurse and wait while Chris pulls the car up to the entrance. We tell her that she doesn't have to stay but, she says it's hospital policy. For the next 20 minutes she stands over the car and watches as we try to securely place Noah in his car seat for the first time. I was too preoccupied to be more than slightly annoyed. Looking back, the nurse was probably laughing as we tried to buckle him up in his swaddle.

After figuring out all the baby-seat mechanisms, and with another deep breath, we began our journey home to Houston. I sit next to my child in the back seat and stare at him. He is sleeping peacefully, totally unaware that I am awestruck. The first thing I do is call my mom and let her know we're on our way. She's been at our house since we left and is a complete nervous wreck.

"Hi Mom! We're heading home with Noah!"

She can now officially plan the welcome home party.

We finish the call and I sit back, thinking of the coincidences that have unfolded these past few days—meeting Melanie, Elizabeth's best friend; my grandmother's birthday engraved on Henry's bracelet; the *Roseanne* cheerleader episode. I stay with that last wink and think to myself, "I wonder what happened to Tom Arnold since the show ended. I haven't seen or heard his name in a very long time." I move to my next thought as we drive through Bastrop on our way to Houston.

We pull into our driveway to find everyone on the front lawn waiting for us. My brother and his kids, Max, Maddie and Ellie, are filming with their iPhones. "Glad someone's getting this," I think, smiling.

I beam with happiness as the door opens. I introduce Noah to his family. My college friends Stephanie, Lisa, and Laura are there to greet me as well. I think one of them was charged with picking up the cake my mom ordered. Appropriately, it had a rainbow on it.

I am floating on clouds. Still in shock that we've made it to this moment I say to myself "What a ride," and try to process the overwhelming experience. Stephanie and Lisa meet me in Noah's room to give me a little remembrance. I open a small box to find a Kate Spade blue and silver bracelet with stars on the outside. The inscription inside reads, "It's in the stars." I start to tear up, give them a hug and exclaim "Yes, indeed. On so many levels."

The next day is full of the same. Friends and family stop by to meet Noah and share their love. Our beautiful first full day at home turns slowly to dusk.

Guests finally depart. I am exhausted and utterly elated. It's getting late but I am still so wound up I can't sleep. I move to the TV room and begin watching one of the late-night shows. It's Jimmy Kimmel. Before he goes to a commercial, he reminds his audience to stay with him. Next up is Tom Arnold. *Wink.*

23

Judgment Day

Six months had to pass before Chris and I would become Noah's parents under Texas law. Up to that point, our agency was the conservator, or guardian of our child and we, as adoptive parents, were responsible for his care. Although technical protocol remained in place during that time period, there was no doubt that we were Noah's parents from the day we brought him home from the hospital. In our eyes, we were family from day one. The judge just sealed the deal.

Anxious to finalize the adoption, we marked the date exactly six months from the day we brought Noah home—September 23, 2015. Chris and I wanted to make sure Noah was ours *forever*. Our family happily caravanned from Houston to San Antonio, enjoyed a celebratory Mexican fiesta lunch and then cheerfully marched to the Bexar County courthouse for our scheduled hearing, Noah leading the way on Grandma Rita's lap as they both enjoyed the ride in her wheelchair. I noticed that the colors of the day appeared much more vibrant than usual. The sky was a brilliant blue, the air was crisp and clear, sweet whiffs of sprinkled sugar cookies followed us, and love and laughter abounded.

We celebrated for many reasons, the first, of course, was Noah becoming ours forever. The second sprung from another coincidence. Moments before we walked into the courtroom, my mother received an astonishing text. Galveston's first municipal swimming pool had just received a million-dollar gift from a donor couple in Atlanta. The Island could now begin construction! My mother had been working on this philanthropy project for years, and she was the first to hear about the funding when it came through—which happened to be seconds before Noah officially became our son.

Some future island residents opened their Galveston water bill and found, stuffed inside, the flyer Chris had designed for my mother's cause requesting donations for the 6-year-old project. They made a whale of a donation that day. The cherry on top was the fact that they happened to be affiliated with a major airline—and flying has been one of Chris's passions since his teenage years. Now that's quite a beautiful Godwink in my book. Actually, two.

24
31

24

365 Days Later

My husband sometimes thinks I share too much. I try to put myself in our birth mother's shoes. If she asks for photos, then I want her to see Noah's development. He's a delight to us, and I hope this gives her pleasure and peace.

Although I enjoy sharing, I was extremely hesitant to send her pictures of Noah's first birthday, afraid that these images would conjure painful memories and swallow her in sorrow. In a compromise with myself, I sent a photo of him thrashing into deliciously sweet cake with his hands and face. I loved this photograph. It was a joy-filled moment captured on film.

I didn't hear back. Uh, oh.

"That's pretty odd," I thought. "She must be so sad, but this day brings me such happiness." I was torn remembering the experience. I knew she must be, too.

That may have been one of the furthest things from her mind. Unbeknownst to me at the time I sent that photo, she was delivering another baby—same day, one year apart. When I heard about this, I started crying all over again. My hands started shaking. I was beside myself with emotion.

Everyone could see me through my glass office walls. I didn't care. I was completely stunned.

How could this happen? Noah now shares his birthday with his half-brother, Benjamin. Wow. This is a lot to take in at one moment. Was this planned? Had to be. What are the chances of this birth date? The thoughts kept pouring through my mind.

Later I was told that she was not induced. Benjamin arrived on this earth exactly one year to the day after Noah's birth. Now that's dharma.

I have come to understand there is an order to life, though I may not comprehend the intricacies as they unfold. I feel that my birth mother and I can now share the joy of this special day for the rest of our lives.

Can I release my sadness now? Yes, I am liberated.

Epilogue

I finish this book as we are just days from my son's third birthday. Time is elusive and expansive and decisive and sometimes even seamless. It feels like we just brought him home from the hospital yesterday.

Sweet moments of us together flash before my eyes. I remember the day I noticed Noah dancing for the first time in his bouncy swing seat. His little feet barely touch the floor, and he is all smiles. *Somewhere Over the Rainbow* by Israel "IZ" Kamakawiwo'ole comes on Pandora and my heart lights up. I turn to find Noah proudly bouncing in rhythm to the lovely melody. How appropriate, I think to myself. It was a magical moment.

Although this book has been rooted in me for some time, it wasn't until Hurricane Harvey hit us in September 2017 that the words flooded out of me. Yes, our home flooded for the first time since it was built in 1963. As water began seeping through the doors and windows, I left a note on Noah's art easel standing in the living room. It read *God bless and protect our home and family*.

Before the water rose to what we feared would be above our heads, we made our way to our neighbor's house, we broke a window and climbed inside to safety on their second floor. Fast forward six months and Chris, Noah and I are still not back in our house. We are, however, safe, protected, and very blessed in another residence where I have had the freedom to let my thoughts flow freely after this life-changing event. It has been extremely cathartic. As a family we've endured some turbulent times. Many might say our adoption journey was pretty painful. It was also pretty great. In retrospect, I see our experience unfold. Our baby was over the rainbow waiting for just the right moment to enter the world. He had to select his birth parents and make sure everyone was in the right alignment. That's not an easy task.

Noah knew what he was doing. He selected his birth parents knowing they would reach out to us. I am sorry there was so much pain in the process, particularly for our birth mother. Noah will grow up knowing that he was our gift from God, through her.

Thank you for letting me share with you. I hope my words bring comfort to you along your path—whatever it is. If you're thinking of adopting, please don't be discouraged. The road to adoption is long and winding, but you will find your way with time. Your baby will be over the rainbow welcoming you home. And you'll see magical, wonderful things along the way. If, incidentally, your path leads you to I-10 in Texas, keep a lookout for a sign for Paw Paw's. Last I checked, it was there.

Acknowledgements

This undertaking began long ago as I began bundling the thoughts percolating in my head onto paper. I would first like to thank my brother, Kenny Herz, for advising me to write without sharing to the world. "Wait until the baby is yours," he cautioned. Without his input to "save it up for later" this book may not have taken root.

Annella Metoyer, thank you for sharing your writing journey and inspiring me to take pen to paper.

Kimberly Kidd, I am grateful we met and partnered through weekend writing retreats. Thank you for being a sounding board these past two years.

Without nudging from my dear friend Victoria Shepherd I wouldn't have included my original notes with our birth parents. Thank you for encouraging me with your kind words and spirit.

Aly Rose, thank you for visiting between your many travels, reading my manuscript and offering your words of wisdom. You gave me confidence to share deeper truths.

To my Mahjong gals: Stephanie Slobin, Karyn Taibel, Dawn Blitz and Wendy Magid—thank you for being a sounding board and support system throughout the adoption process, Hurricane Harvey, and writing of this book.

I would like to thank everyone who read my original manuscript and provided much needed feedback—or silence. Both avenues gave me much to contemplate and led to a stronger finished product: Frank Billingsley, Judy Olson, Katherine Otte, Rory Hall, Danielle Kruger, Caroline Schlemmer, Carol Kadison, Bret Kadison, Brandi Brown, Amy Krasner, Ariana Rose Komaroff and Cindy Young.

Thank you Zak Kadison for not just reading my manuscript—but dissecting it, giving me helpful guidelines for storytelling, and encouraging me to change the name of my book. I am also grateful for your introduction to my amazing editor Joshua Weinstein.

Joshua Wienstein—you are a literary rock star and word wizard. Thank you for providing much needed guidance to this neophyte writer. You pulled out the best in me. Your wit and wisdom helped me cross the finish line.

John Hodgkinson and Denise Cassino, I offer exponential gratitude for your mentorship through this long and winding undertaking. Your guidance through formatting, publishing and publicity has been truly appreciated.

To my parents BJ and Buddy Herz, I love you for bringing me into this world and helping me grow into the woman, wife and mother I am today. I feel very blessed to be your daughter.

None of this could have taken place without the love, support and guidance from my husband Chris. Thank you for believing in my dream and encouraging me to write this story. Thank you for your beautiful sketches that grace this book. Thank you for entering my world at the perfect time. My cup runneth over with you and Noah in my life.

I invite you to share your journey of grit and magic
on Instagram: #mygritandmagic and
connect through my website at
www.melanieherzpromecene.com

#MyGritAndMagic

SHARE *on* INSTAGRAM

About Author
Melanie Herz Promecene

Melanie Herz Promecene lives in Houston, Texas with her husband Chris and son Noah. She is a fifth generation Galveston BOI and graduate of The University of Texas at Austin and Parsons School of Design. Melanie currently works as the Director of Interiors for a full-service design firm and enjoys creating beautiful spaces for people to live, work and play. She loves entertaining family and friends, exploring the arts through travel and understanding the universal human experience. Melanie's favorite past time is discovering the world through her son's eyes.

CPSIA information can be obtained
at www.ICGtesting.com
Printed in the USA
LVHW010001030320
648717LV00017B/603

9 781641 842815